APPLAUSE FIRST FOLIO EDITIONS

Twelfe Night, Or What you will

BY

William Shakespeare

PREPARED & ANNOTATED BY

NEIL FREEMAN

APPLAUSE
NEW YORK • LONDON

The Applause Shakespeare Library

Folio Texts

AN APPLAUSE ORIGINAL

Twelfe Night, or What you will

original concept devised by Neil Freeman

original research computer entry by Margaret McBride

original software programmes designed and developed by
James McBride and Terry Lim

Text layout designed and executed by Neil Freeman

Some elements of this text were privately published under the collective title of
The Freeman–Nichols Folio Scripts 1991–96

ISBN: 1-55783-380-X

Library of Congress Cataloging-in-Publication Data

Library of Congress Catalog Card Number: 99-65415

British Library Cataloging-in-Publication Data

A catalogue record of this book is available from the British Library

APPLAUSE BOOKS

1841 Broadway Suite 1100	Combined Book Services Ltd.
New York, NY 10023	Units I/K Paddock Wood Dist. Ctr.
Phone (212) 765-7880	Paddock Wood,
Fax: (212) 765-7875	Tonbridge Kent TN12 6UU
	Phone 0189 283-7171
	Fax 0189 283-7272

Printed in Canada

CONTENTS

ACKNOWLEDGEMENTS

My grateful thanks to all who have helped in the growth and development of this work. Special thanks to Norman Welsh who first introduced me to the Folio Text, and to Tina Packer who (with Kristin Linklater and all the members of Shakespeare & Co.) allowed me to explore the texts on the rehearsal floor. To Jane Nichols for her enormous generosity in providing the funding which allowed the material to be computerised. To James and Margaret McBride and Terry Lim for their expertise, good humour and hard work. To the National Endowment for the Arts for their award of a Major Artist Fellowship and to York University for their award of the Joseph G. Green Fellowship. To actors, directors and dramaturgs at the Stratford Festival, Ontario; Toronto Free Theatre (that was); the Skylight Theatre, Toronto and Tamanhouse Theatre of Vancouver. To colleagues, friends and students at The University of British Columbia, Vancouver; York University, Toronto; Concordia University, Montreal; The National Theatre School of Canada in Montreal; Equity Showcase Theatre, Toronto; The Centre for Actors Study and Training (C.A.S.T.), Toronto; The National Voice Intensive at Simon Fraser University, Vancouver; Studio 58 of Langara College, Vancouver; Professional Workshops in the Arts, Vancouver; U.C.L.A., Los Angeles; Loyola Marymount, Los Angeles; San Jose State College, California; Long Beach State College, California; Brigham Young University, Utah, and Hawaii; Holy Cross College, Massachussetts; Guilford College, North Carolina. To Chairman John Wright and Associate Dean Don Paterson for their incredible personal support and encouragement. To Rachel Ditor and Tom Scholte for their timely research assistance. To Alan and Chris Baker, and Stephanie McWilliams for typographical advice. To Jay L. Halio, Hugh Richmond, and G.B. Shand for their critical input. To the overworked and underpaid proofreading teams of Ron Oten and Yuuattee Tanipersaud, Patrick Galligan and Leslie Barton, Janet Van De Graaff and Angela Dorhman (with input from Todd Sandomirsky, Bruce Alexander Pitkin, Catelyn Thornton and Michael Roberts). And above all to my wife Julie, for her patient encouragement, courteous advice, critical eye and long sufferance!

SPECIAL ACKNOWLEDGEMENTS

Paul Sugarman and Glenn Young of Applause Books; Houghton Mifflin Company for permission to quote from the line numbering system developed for *The Riverside Shakespeare*: Evans, Gwynne Blakemore, Harry Levin, Anne Barton, Herschel Baker, Frank Kermode, Hallet D. Smith, and Marie Edel, editors, *The Riverside Shakespeare*. Copyright © 1974 by Houghton Mifflin Company.

DEFINITIONS OF AND GUIDE TO PHOTOGRAPHIC COPIES OF THE EARLY TEXTS

(see Appendix A for a brief history of the First Folio, the Quartos, and their uneasy relationship with modern texts)

A QUARTO (Q)

A single text, so called because of the book size resulting from a particular method of printing. Eighteen of Shakespeare's plays were published in this format by different publishers at various dates between 1594–1622 prior to the appearance of the 1623 Folio. Of the eighteen quarto texts, scholars suggest that fourteen have value as source texts. An extremely useful collection of them is to be found in Michael J. B. Allen and Kenneth Muir, eds., *Shakespeare's Plays in Quarto* (Berkeley: University of California Press, 1981).

THE FIRST FOLIO (F1)[1]

Thirty-six of Shakespeare's plays (excluding *Pericles* and *Two Noble Kinsmen,* in which he had a hand) appeared in one volume published in 1623. All books of this size were termed Folios, again because of the sheet size and printing method, hence this volume is referred to as the First Folio; two recent photographic editions of the work are:

Charlton Hinman, ed., *The Norton Facsimile (The First Folio of Shakespeare)* (1968; republished New York: W. W. Norton & Company, Inc., 1996).

Helge Kökeritz, ed., *Mr. William Shakespeare's Comedies, Histories & Tragedies* (New Haven: Yale University Press, 1954).

THE SECOND FOLIO (F2)

Scholars suggest that the Second Folio, dated 1632 but perhaps not published until 1640, has little authority, especially since it created hundreds of new problematical readings of its own. Nevertheless, more than eight hundred modern text readings can be attributed to it. The most recent reproduction is D. S. Brewer, ed., *Mr.*

---

[1]   For a full overview of the First Folio see the monumental two-volume work: Charlton Hinman, *The Printing and Proof Reading of the First Folio of Shakespeare* (2 volumes) (Oxford: Clarendon Press, 1963) and W. W. Greg, *The Editorial Problem in Shakespeare: a Survey of the Foundations of the Text,* 3rd. ed. (Oxford: Clarendon Press, 1954); for a brief summary, see the forty-six page publication from Peter W. M. Blayney, *The First Folio of Shakespeare* (Washington, DC: Folger Library Publications, 1991).

William Shakespeare's Comedies, Histories & Tragedies, the Second Folio Reproduced in Facsimile (Dover, NH: Boydell & Brewer Ltd., 1985).

The Third Folio (1664) and the Fourth Folio (1685) have even less authority, and are rarely consulted except in cases of extreme difficulty.

THE THIRD FOLIO (F3)

The Third Folio, carefully proofed (though apparently not against the previous edition) takes great pains to correct anomalies in punctuation ending speeches and in expanding abbreviations. It also introduced seven new plays supposedly written by Shakespeare, only one of which, *Pericles*, has been established as such. The most recent reproduction is D. S. Brewer, ed., *Mr. William Shakespeare's Comedies, Histories & Tragedies, the Third Folio Reproduced in Facsimile* (Dover, NH: Boydell & Brewer Ltd., 1985).

THE FOURTH FOLIO (F4)

Paradoxically, while the Fourth Folio was the most carefully edited of all, its concentration on grammatical clarity and ease of comprehension by its readers at the expense of faithful reproduction of F1 renders it the least useful for those interested in the setting down on paper of Elizabethan theatre texts. The most recent reproduction is D. S. Brewer, ed., *Mr. William Shakespeare's Comedies, Histories & Tragedies, the Fourth Folio Reproduced in Facsimile* (Dover, NH: Boydell & Brewer Ltd., 1985).

WELCOME TO THESE SCRIPTS

These scripts are designed to do three things:

1. show the reader what the First Folio (often referred to as F1) set down on paper, rather than what modern editions think ought to have been set down

2. provide both reader and theatre practitioner an easy journey through some of the information the original readers might have garnered from F1 and other contemporary scripts which is still relevant today

3. provide a simple way for readers to see not only where modern texts alter the First Folio, and how, but also allow readers to explore both First Folio and modern versions of the disputed passage without having to turn to an Appendix or a different text

all this, hopefully without interfering with the action of the play.

What the First Folio sets on paper will be the basis for what you see. In the body of the play-text that follows, the words (including spellings and capitalisations), the punctuation (no matter how ungrammatical), the structure of the lines (including those moments of peculiar verse or unusual prose), the stage directions, the act and scene divisions, and (for the most part) the prefixes used for each character will be as set in the First Folio.

In addition, new, on page, visual symbols specially devised for these texts will help point out both the major stepping stones in the Elizabethan debate/rhetorical process contained in the plays (a fundamental part of understanding both the inner nature of each character as well as the emotional clashes between them), and where and how (and sometimes why) modern texts have altered the First Folio information. And, unlike any other script, opposite each page of text will be a blank page where readers can make their own notes and commentary.

However, there will be the rare occasion when these texts do not exactly follow the First Folio.

Sometimes F1's **words or phrases** are meaningless; for example, the lovely misprinting of 'which' in *Twelfth Night* as 'wh?ch', or in *Romeo and Juliet* the type-setting corruptions of 'speeh' for 'speech' and the running of the two words 'not away' as 'notaway'. If there are no alternative contemporary texts (a Quarto version of the play) or if no modification was made by any of the later Folios (The Second Folio of 1632, The Third Folio of 1664, or The Fourth Folio of 1685, termed F2, F3, and F4 respectively) then the F1 printing will be set as is, no matter how peculiar, and the modern correction footnoted. However, if a more appropriate alternative is available in a Quarto (often referred to as Q) or F2, F3, or F4, that 'correction' will be set directly into the text, replacing the F1 reading, and footnoted accordingly, as in the case of 'wh?ch', 'speeh', and 'notaway'.

The only time F1's **punctuation** will be altered is when the original setting is so blurred that an accurate deciphering of what F1 set cannot be determined. In such cases, alternative punctuation from F2–4 or Q will be set and a footnote will explain why.

The only time F1's **line structure** will not be followed is when at the end of a very long line, the final word or part of the word cannot fit onto the single line, nor be set as a new line in F1 because of the text that follows and is therefore set above or below the original line at the right hand side of the column. In such rare cases these texts will complete the line as a single line, and mark it with a † to show the change from F1. In all other cases, even when in prose F1 is forced to split the final word of a speech in half, and set only a few letters of it on a new line—for example in *Henry the Fifth*, Pistoll's name is split as 'Pi' on one line and 'stoll' (as the last part of the speech) on the next—these texts will show F1 exactly as set.

Some liberties have to be taken with the **prefixes** (the names used at the beginning of speeches to show the reader which character is now speaking), for Ff (all the Folios) and Qq (all the Quartos) are not always consistent. Sometimes slightly different abbreviations are used for the same character—in *The Tempest,* King Alonso is variously referred to as 'Al.', 'Alo.', 'Alon.', and 'Alonso'. Sometimes the same abbreviation is used for two different characters—in *A Midsummer Nights Dream* the characters Quince, the 'director' and author of the Mechanicals play, and Titania, Queen of the fairies, are given the same abbreviation 'Qu.'. While in this play common sense can distinguish what is intended, the confusions in *Julius Caesar* between Lucius and Lucullus, each referred to sometimes as 'Luc.', and in *The Comedy of Errors,* where the twin brothers Antipholus are both abbreviated to 'Antiph.', cannot be so easily sorted out. Thus, whereas F1 will show a variety of abbreviated prefixes, these texts will usually choose just one complete name per character and stay with it throughout.

However, there are certain cases where one full name will not suffice. Sometimes F1 will change the prefix for a single character from scene to scene, the change usually reflecting the character's new function or status. Thus in *The Comedy of Errors,* as a drinking companion of the local Antipholus, the goldsmith Angelo is referred to by his given name 'Ang.', but once business matters go awry he very quickly becomes a businessman, referred to as 'Gold'. Similar changes affect most of the characters in *A Midsummer Nights Dream,* and a complex example can be found in *Romeo and Juliet.* While modern texts give Juliet's mother the single prefix Lady Capulet throughout (incorrectly since neither she nor Capulet are named as aristocrats anywhere in the play) both Ff and Qq refer to her in a wonderful character-revealing multiplicity of ways—Mother, Capulet Wife, Lady, and Old Lady—a splendid gift for actress, director, designer, and reader alike.

Surprisingly, no modern text ever sets any of these variations. Believing such changes integral to the development of the characters so affected, these texts will. In such cases, each time the character's prefix changes the new prefix will be set, and a small notation alongside the prefix (either by reference to the old name, or by adding the symbol •) will remind the reader to whom it refers.

Also, some alterations will be made to F1's **stage directions,** not to the words themselves or when they occur, but to the way they are going to be presented visually. Scholars agree F1 contains two different types of stage direction: those that came in the original manuscript from which the Playhouse copy of the play was made, and a second set that were added in for theatrical clarification by the Playhouse. The scholars conjecture that the literary or manuscript directions, presumably from Shakespeare, mainly dealing with entries and key actions such as battles, are those that F1 sets centred on a separate line, while the additional Playhouse directions, usually dealing with offstage sounds, music, and exits, are those F1 sets alongside the spoken dialogue, usually flush against the right hand side of the column. In performance terms there seems to be a useful distinction between the two, though this is only a rule of thumb. The centred manuscript (Shakespearean?) directions tend to stop or change the action of the play, that is, the scene is affected by the action the direction demands, whereas the Playhouse directions (to the side of the text) serve to underscore what is already taking place. (If a word is needed to distinguish the two, the centred directions can be called 'action' directions, because they are events in and of themselves, while the side-set directions could be called 'supportive' or 'continuous' since they tend not to distract from the current onstage action.)

Since F1 seems to visually distinguish between the two types (setting them on different parts of the page) and there seems to be a logical theatrical differentiation as to both the source and function of each, it seems only appropriate that these scripts also mark the difference between them. Both Ff and Qq's side-set directions are often difficult to decipher while reading the text: sometimes they are set so close to the spoken text they get muddled up with it, despite the different typeface, and oftentimes have to be abbreviated to fit in. These are drawbacks shared by most modern texts. Thus these texts will distinguish them in a slightly different way (see p. xxvi below).

Finally, there will be two occasional alterations to Ff's **fonts.** F1 used **italics** for a large number of different purposes, sometimes creating confusion on the page. What these texts will keep as italics are letters, poems, songs, and the use of foreign languages. What they will not set in italics are real names, prefixes, and stage directions. Also at the top of each play, and sometimes at the beginning of a letter or poem, F1 would set a large wonderfully **decorative opening letter,** with the second letter of the word being capitalised, the style tying in with the borders that surrounded the opening and closing of each play. Since these texts will not be reproducing the decorative borders, the decorative letters won't be set either.

MAKING FULL USE OF THESE TEXTS

WHAT MODERN CHANGES WILL BE SHOWN

WORDS AND PHRASES

Modern texts often tidy up F1's words and phrases. Real names, both of people and places, and foreign languages are often reworked for modern understanding; for example, the French town often set in F1 as 'Callice' is usually reset as 'Calais'. Modern texts 'correct' the occasional Elizabethan practice of setting a singular noun with plural verb (and vice versa), as well as the infrequent use of the past tense of a verb to describe a current situation. These texts will set the F1 reading, and footnote the modern corrections whenever they occur.

More problematical are the possibilities of choice, especially when a Q and F version of the same play show a different reading for the same line and either choice is valid—even more so when both versions are offered by different modern texts. Juliet's 'When I shall die,/Take him and cut him out in little starres' offered by Ff/Q1-3 being offset by Q4's 'When he shall die...' is a case in point. Again, these texts will set the F1 reading, and footnote the alternatives.

LINE STRUCTURE CHANGES RELATED TO PROBLEMS OF 'CASTING-OFF'

The First Folio was usually prepared in blocks of twelve pages at a time. Six pairs of pages would be prepared, working both forward and backward simultaneously. Thus from the centre of any twelve-page block, pages six and seven were set first, then five and eight, then four and nine, then three and ten, then two and eleven, and finally one and twelve. This meant each compositor had to work out very carefully how much copy would fit not only each sheet, but also how much would be needed overall to reach the outer edges of pages one and twelve to match it to the previously set text, (prior to page one) or about to be set text (after page twelve). Naturally the calculations weren't always accurate. Sometimes there was too little text left for too great a space: in such cases, if the manuscript were set as it should have been, a great deal of empty paper would be left free, a condition often described as 'white' space. Sometimes too much text remained for too small a space, and if the manuscript were to be set according to its normal layout, every available inch would be taken up with type (and even then the text might not fit), a condition that could be described as 'crammed space'.

Essentially, this created a huge design problem, and most commentators suggest when it arose the printing house policy was to sacrifice textual accuracy to neatness of design. Thus, so the argument goes, in the case of white space, extra lines of type would have to be created where (presumably) none originally existed. *Hamlet* provides an excellent example with the Polonius speech 'Indeed that's out of the air' starting at line 78 of what most modern texts term Act Two Scene 2. Q2 sets the four-line speech as prose, and most modern texts follow suit. However, F1, faced with a potentially huge white space problem at the bottom of the right hand column of p. 261 in the Tragedy section, resets the speech as eleven lines of very irregular verse! In the case of crammed space, five lines of verse might suddenly become three lines of prose, or in one very severe case of overcrowding in *Henry The Fourth Part Two,* words, phrases, and even half lines of text might be omitted to reduce the text sufficiently.

When such cases occur, this text will set F1 as shown, and the modern texts' suggested alternatives will be footnoted and discussed.

LINE STRUCTURE CHANGES NOT RELATED TO PROBLEMS OF 'CASTING-OFF'

In addition, modern texts regularly make changes to F1's line structure which are not related to 'white' or 'crammed' space, often to the detriment of both character and scene. Two major reasons are offered for the changes.

First, either (a few) prose lines suddenly appear in what essentially is a verse scene (or a few verse lines in a sea of prose) and the modern texts, feeling the scene should be standardised, restructure the offending lines accordingly. *The Tempest* is atrociously served this way[2], for where F1, the only source text, shows the conspirators Caliban, Stephano, and, very occasionally, Trinculo, speaking verse as well as prose even within the same speech (a sure sign of personal striving and inner disturbance) most modern texts readjust the lines to show only Caliban speaking verse (dignifying him more than he deserves) and Stephano and Trinculo only speaking prose (thus robbing them of their dangerous flights of fancy).

Second, some Ff verse lines appear so appallingly defective in terms of their rhythm and length that modern texts feel it necessary to make a few 'readjustments' of the lines around them to bring the offending lines back to a coherent, rhythmic whole. Many of the later plays are abominably served in this regard: in *Macbeth,* for example, over a hundred F1 passages involving more than 200 lines (90 percent of which were set by the usually reliable compositor A) have been altered by most modern texts. Most of these changes concentrate on regularising moments where a character is under tremendous upheaval and hardly likely to be speaking pure formal verse at that particular moment!

These changes come about through a mistaken application of modern grammat-

---

[2]   Commentators suggest the copy play used for setting F1, coming from Stratford as it did, and thus unsupervised by Shakespeare in the Playhouse preparation of the document, prepared by Ralph Crane, was at times defective, especially in distinguishing clearly between verse and prose: this is why most modern texts do not follow F1's choices in these dubious passages: readers are invited to explore *The Tempest* within this series, especially the footnotes, as a theatrical vindication of the original F1 setting

ical considerations to texts that were originally prepared not according to grammar but rhetoric. One of rhetoric's many strengths is that it can show not only when characters are in self-control but also when they are not. In a rhetorically set passage, the splutters of a person going through an emotional breakdown, as with Othello, can be shown almost verbatim, with peculiar punctuations, spellings, breaks, and all. If the same passage were to be set grammatically it would be very difficult to show the same degree of personal disintegration on the printed page.[3] F1's occasional weird shifts between verse and prose and back again, together with the moments of extreme linear breakdown, are the equivalents of human emotional breakdown, and once the anomalies of Elizabethan script preparation are accounted for,[4] the rhetorical breakdowns on F1's printed page are clear indications of a character's disintegration within the play. When modern texts tidy up such blemishes grammatically they unwittingly remove essential theatrical and/or character clues for reader and theatre person alike:

In these texts, F1's line structure will be set as is, and all such modern alterations (prose to verse, verse to prose, regularisation of originally unmetrical lines) will be shown. The small symbol ° will be added to show where modern texts suggest a line should end rather than where F1 shows it does. A thin vertical line will be set to the left alongside any text where the modern texts have converted F1's prose to verse, or vice versa. The more large-scale of these changes will be boxed for quicker reader recognition. Most of these changes will be footnoted in the text where they occur, and a comparison of the two different versions of the text and what each could signify theatrically will be offered. For examples of both, see p. xxiii below.

The Special Problems Affecting What Are Known As 'Shared' or 'Split' Verse Lines

A definition, and their importance to the Shakespeare texts

Essentially, split lines are short lines of verse which, when placed together, form the equivalent of a full verse line. Most commentators suggest they are very useful in speeding the play along, for the second character (whose line attaches on to the end of the first short line) is expected to use the end of the first character's line as a

---

[3] For a full discussion of this, readers are directed to Neil Freeman, *Shakespeare's First Texts* (Vancouver: Folio Scripts, 1994).

[4] Readers are referred to an excellent chapter by Gary Taylor which analyses the whole background, conjectural and known, concerning the preparation of the first scripts. He points out the pitfalls of assuming the early texts as sole authority for all things Shakespearean: he examines the conjectured movement of the scripts from Shakespeare's pen to printed edition, and carefully examples the changes and alterations that could occur, (most notably at the hands of the manuscript copyists), as well as the interferences and revampings of the Playhouse, plus the effects of the first typesetters' personal habits and carelessness. Stanley Wells and Gary Taylor, *William Shakespeare: A Textual Companion* (Oxford: Clarendon Press, 1987), 1–68.

springboard and jump in with an immediate reply, enhancing the quickness of the debate. Thus in *Measure for Measure*, Act Two Scene 2, modern ll. 8–10, the Provost, trying to delay Claudio's execution, has asked Angelo whether Claudio has to die the following day: Angelo's questioning affirmation ends with a very pointed short line, followed immediately by a short line opening from the Provost.

Angelo	Did I not tell thee yea? hadst thou not order? Why do'st thou aske againe?
Provost	Lest I might be too rash: Under your good correction, I have seene When after execution ...

If the Provost replies immediately after, or just as, Angelo finishes, an explosive dramatic tension is created. Allowing a minor delay before reply, as many actors do, will reduce the impact of the moment, and create a hesitation where one probably does not exist.

The occasional problem

So far so good. But the problems start when more than two short lines follow each other. If there are three short lines in succession, which should be joined, #1 and #2, or #2 and #3? Later in the same scene, Claudio's sister Isabella has, at the insistence of Claudio's friend Lucio, come to plead with Angelo for her brother's life. In Lucio's eyes she is giving up too easily, hence the following (modern ll. 45–49):

Lucio	You are too cold: if you should need a pin, You could not with more tame a tongue desire it: To him, I say.
Isabella	Must he needs die?
Angelo	Maiden, no remedie?

And here it seems fairly obvious Isabella and Angelo's lines should join together, thus allowing a wonderful dramatic pause following Lucio's urging before Isabella plucks up enough courage to try. Most modern texts set the lines accordingly, with Lucio's the short odd line out.

But what about the three lines contained in the exchange that follows almost straightaway?

Isabella	But you might doe't & do the world no wrong If so your heart were touch'd with that remorse, As mine is to him?
Angelo	Hee's sentenc'd, tis too late.
Lucio	You are too cold.
Isabella	Too late? why no: I that doe speak a word

> May call it againe: well, beleeve this
>   (modern line numbering 53–56)

Does Angelo's 'Hee's sentenc'd...' spring off Isabella's line, leaving Isabella speechless and turning to go before Lucio urges her on again? Or does Angelo pause (to frame a reply?) before speaking, leaving Lucio to quickly jump in quietly giving Isabella no time to back off? Either choice is possible, and dramatically valid. And readers should be allowed to make their own choice, which automatically means each reader should able to see the possibility of such choices when they occur.

The problem magnified by the way modern texts set split/shared lines

However, because of a peculiarity faced by the modern texts not shared by Ff/Qq, modern texts rarely show such possibilities to their readers but make the choice for them. The peculiarity comes about from a change in text layout initiated in the eighteenth century.

Ff/Qq always set short lines directly under one another, as shown in the examples above. In 1778 George Steevens, a highly respected editor, started to show split lines a new way, by advancing the second split line to just beyond where the first split line finishes, viz.

Angelo	Did I not tell thee yea? hadst thou not order?
	Why do'st thou aske againe?
Provost	Lest I might be too rash:
	Under your good correction, I have seene
	When after execution...

Since that date all editions of Shakespeare have followed this practice, which is fine as long as there are only two short lines, but when three follow each other, a choice has to be made. Thus the second Isabella/Angelo/Lucio sequence could be set as either

Isabella	But you might doe't & do the world no wrong
	If so your heart were touch'd with that remorse,
	As mine is to him?
Angelo	Hee's sentenc'd, tis too late.
Lucio	You are too cold.
Isabella	Too late? why no: I that doe speak a word
	May call it againe: well, beleeve this...

(the usual modern choice), or

Isabella	But you might doe't & do the world no wrong
	If so your heart were touch'd with that remorse,
	As mine is to him?

Angelo	Hee's sentenc'd, tis too late.
Lucio	You are too cold.
Isabella	Too late? why no: I that doe speak a word
	May call it againe: well, beleeve this . . .

This modern typesetting convention has robbed the reader of a very important moment of choice. Indeed, at the beginning of the twentieth century, Richard Flatter[5] suggested that what modern commentators consider to be split lines may not be split lines at all. He offers two other suggestions: pauses and hesitations could exist between each line, or the lines could in fact be spoken one on top of another, a very important consideration for the crowd responses to Anthony in the funeral scene of *Julius Caesar*. Either way, the universally adopted Steevens layout precludes the reader/theatre practitioner from even seeing such possibilities.

These texts will show the F1 layout as is, and will indicate via footnote when a choice is possible (in the case of three short lines, or more, in succession) and by the symbol } when the possibility of springboarding exists. Thus the Folio Texts would show the first Angelo/Provost example as:

Angelo	Did I not tell thee yea? hadst thou not order?
	Why do'st thou aske againe?
	}
Provost	Lest I might be too rash:
	Under your good correction, I have seene
	When after execution . . .

In nearly all cases the } shows where most modern texts insist on setting a shared split line. However, readers are cautioned that in many of the later plays, the single line so created is much longer than pentameter, and often very a-rhythmic. In such cases the lines could have great value as originally set (two separate short lines), especially when a key debate is in process (for example, *Measure for Measure, The Tragedie of Cymbeline, Othello,* and *The Winters Tale*).

THE UNUSUAL SINGLE SPLIT LINE (PLEASE SEE 'A CAVEAT', P. XXXVIII)

So far the discussion has centred on short lines shared by two or more characters. Ff/Qq offer another complication rarely, if ever, accepted by most modern texts. Quite often, and not because of white space, a single character will be given two consecutive short lines within a single speech. *Romeo and Juliet* is chock full of this device: in the famous balcony scene (modern texts numbering 2.2.62–3) Juliet asks Romeo

How cam'st thou hither.

---

5   Richard Flatter, *Shakespeare's Producing Hand* (London: Heinemann, 1948, reprint).

> Tell me, and wherefore?
> The Orchard walls are high, and hard to climbe

The first two lines (five syllables each) suggest a minute pause between them as Juliet hesitates before asking the all important second line (with its key second part 'and wherefore'). Since Qq rarely set such 'single split lines' most modern texts refuse to set any of them, but combine them:

> How cams't thou hither. Tell me and wherefore?

This basically F1 device is set by all the compositors and followed by all other Folios. This text will follow suit, highlighting them with the symbol → for quick recognition, viz.:

> How cam'st thou hither. →
> Tell me, and wherefore?
> The Orchard walls are high, and hard to climbe

SENTENCE AND PUNCTUATION STRUCTURES

A CHARACTER'S THOUGHTFUL & EMOTIONAL JOURNEY

A quick comparison between these texts and both the Ff/Qq's and the modern texts will reveal two key differences in the layout of the dialogue on the printed page—the bolding of major punctuation, and the single line dropping of text whenever a new sentence begins.

The underlying principle behind these texts is that since the handwritten documents from which they stem were originally intended for the actor and Playhouse, in addition to their poetical values, the Ff/Qq scripts represent a theatrical process. Even if the scripts are being read just for pleasure, at the back of the reader's mind should be the notion of characters on a stage and actors acting (and the word 'process' rather than 'practice' is deliberate, with process suggesting a progression, development, or journey).

The late Jean-Louis Barrault gave a wonderful definition of acting, and of this journey, suggesting an actor's job was to strive to remain in 'the ever-changing present'. If something happens onstage (an entry, an exit, a verbal acceptance or denial of what the actor's character has suggested), the 'present' has changed, and the character must readjust accordingly. Just as onstage, the actor should be prepared for the character to re-adjust, and in rehearsal should be examining how and why it does, so should the reader in the library, armchair, or classroom.

In many ways, the key to Shakespeare is discovering how each character's mind works; perceiving the emotions and intellects as they act and react helps the reader understand from where the poetical imagination and utterance stem.

Certain elements of each character's emotional and intellectual journey, and where it changes, are encoded into the sentence structure of Ff/Qq.

Elizabethan education prepared any schooled individual (via the 'petty school' and the private tutor) for the all important and essential daily rough and tumble of argument and debate. Children were trained not only how to frame an argument so as to win it hands down, but also how to make it entertaining so as to enthrall the neutral listener.

The overall training, known as 'rhetoric', essentially allowed intellect and emotion to exist side by side, encouraging the intellect to keep the emotion in check. The idea was not to deny the emotions, but ensure they didn't swamp the 'divinity' of reason, the only thing separating man from beast. While the initial training was mainly vocal, any written matter of the period automatically reflected the ebb and flow of debate. What was set on the printed page was not grammar, but a representation of the rhetorical process.

DROPPING A LINE TO ILLUSTRATE F1'S SENTENCE STRUCTURE

Put at its simplest, in any document of the period, each sentence would represent a new intellectual and emotional stage of a rhetorical argument. When this stage of the argument was completed, a period would be set (occasionally a question mark or, much more rarely, an exclamation mark—both followed by a capital letter) signifying the end of that stage of the argument, and the beginning of the next.

Thus in the First Folio, the identification of each new sentence is an automatic (and for us, four hundred years later, a wonderful) aid to understanding how a character is reacting to and dealing with Barrault's ever-changing present.

To help the reader quickly spot the new steppingstone in an argument, and thus the point of transition, these texts highlight where one sentence ends and the new one begins by simply dropping a line whenever a new sentence starts. Thus the reader has a visual reminder that the character is making a transition to deal with a change in the current circumstances of the scene (or in the process of self-discovery in the case of soliloquies).

This device has several advantages. The reader can instantly see where the next step in the argument begins. The patterns so created on the page can quickly illuminate whenever a contrast between characters' thought patterns occurs. (Sometimes the sentences are short and precise, suggesting the character is moving quickly from one idea to the next. Sometimes the sentences are very long, suggesting the character is undergoing a very convoluted process. Sometimes the sentences contain nothing but facts, suggesting the character has no time to entertain; sometimes they are filled with high-flown imagery, perhaps suggesting the character is trying to mask a very weak argument with verbal flummery.) The patterns can also show when a character's style changes within itself, say from long and convoluted to short and precise, or vice versa. It can also immediately pinpoint when a character is in trouble and not arguing coherently or logically, something modern texts often alter out of grammatical necessity.

With patience, all this could be gleaned from the modern texts (in as far as they set the Ff sentence structure, which they often don't) and from a photostat of the First Folio, by paying special attention to where the periods are set. But there is one extra very special advantage to this new device of dropping a line: this has to do once more with the Elizabethan method of setting down spoken argument on paper, especially when the character speaking is not in the best of all possible worlds.

If an Elizabethan person/character is arguing well, neatly, cleanly, tidily, then a printed representation of that argument would also be clean, neat, and tidy—to modern eyes it would be grammatically acceptable. If the same character is emotionally upset, or incapable of making a clear and tidy argument, then the on-paper representation would be muddy and untidy—to modern eyes totally ungrammatical and often not acceptable. By slightly isolating each sentence these texts very quickly allow the reader to spot when a sentence's construction is not all that it should be, say in the middle of Viola's so-called ring speech in *Twelfth Night* (Act Two Scene 2), or Helena's declaration of love for Bertram in *All's Well That Ends Well* (Act One Scene 3), or the amazing opening to *As You Like It,* where Orlando's opening litany of complaint against his brother starts with a single sentence twenty lines long.

This is especially relevant when a surprising modern editorial practice is accounted for. Very often the Ff sentence structures are markedly altered by modern texts, especially when the Ff sentences do not seem 'grammatical'—thus Orlando's twenty-line monster is split into six separate, grammatically correct sentences by all modern texts. And then there is the case of Shylock in *The Merchant of Venice,* a Jewish man being goaded and tormented beyond belief by the very Christians who helped his daughter elope with a Christian, taking a large part of Shylock's fortune with her. A sentence comparison of the famous Act Three Scene 1 speech culminating in 'Hath not a Jew eyes?' is very instructive. All modern texts set the speech as between fifteen and seventeen sentences in length: whatever the pain, anger, and personal passion, the modern texts encourage dignity and self-control, a rational Shylock. But this is a Shylock completely foreign to both Q1 and Ff. Q1 show the same speech as only four sentences long, Ff five—a veritable onflow of intellect and passion all mixed together, all unstoppable for the longest period of time—a totally different being from that shown by the modern texts. What is more, this is a totally different Shylock from the one seen earlier in the Ff/Q1 version of the play, where, even in the extremes of discomfort with the old enemy Anthonio, his sentence structures are rhetorically balanced and still grammatical to modern eyes.

Here, with Shylock, there are at least three benefits to dropping the sentence: the unusualness of the speech is immediately spotted; the change in style between this and any of his previous speeches can be quickly seen; and, above all, the moment where the speech moves from a long unchecked outpouring to a quick series of brief, dangerously rational sentences can be quickly identified. And these advantages will be seen in such changed sentence circumstances in any play in any of these texts.

THE HIGHLIGHTING OF THE MAJOR PUNCTUATION IN THESE TEXTS

A second key element of rhetoric encoded into the Ff/Qq texts clearly shows the characters' mind in action. The encoding lies in the remaining punctuation which, unlike much modern punctuation, serves a double function, one dealing with the formation of the thought, the other with the speaking of it.

Apart from the period, dealt with already, essentially there are two sets of punctuation to consider, minor and major, each with their own very specific functions.

Shakespearean characters reflect the mode of thinking of their time. Elizabethans were trained to constantly add to or modify thoughts. They added a thought to expand the one already made. They denied the first thought so as to set up alternatives. They elaborated a thought so as to clarify what has already been said. They suddenly moved into splendid puns or non-sequiturs (emotional, logical, or both) because they had been immediately stimulated by what they or others had just said. The **minor punctuation** (essentially the comma [,] the parenthesis or bracket [( )], and the dash) reflects all this.

In establishing thought processes for each character, minor punctuation shows every new nuance of thought: every tiny punctuation in this category helps establish the deftness and dance of each character's mind. In *As You Like It* (Act Three Scene 2, modern line numbering 400–402) the Ff setting of Rosalind's playing with her beloved Orlando has a wonderful coltish exuberance as she runs rings round his protestations of love:

> Love is meerely a madnesse, and I tel you,
> deserves as well a darke house,* and a whip,* as madmen do:

Her mind is adding extra thoughts as she goes: the Ff commas are as much part of her spirit and character as the words are—though most modern texts create a much more direct essayist, preaching what she already knows, by removing the two Ff commas marked *.[6]

A similar situation exists with Macbeth, facing Duncan whom he must kill if he is

---

[6] Unfortunately, many modern texts eradicate the F and Q minor punctuation arguing the need for light (or infrequent) punctuation to preserve the speed of speech. This is not necessarily helpful, since what it removes is just a new thought marker, not an automatic indication to pause: too often the result is that what the first texts offer a character as a series of closely-worked out dancing thought-patterns (building one quick thought—as marked by a comma—on top of another) is turned into a series of much longer phrases: often, involved and reactive busy minds are artificially turned into (at best) eloquent ones, suddenly capable of perfect and lengthy rationality where the situation does not warrant such a reaction, or (at worst) vapid ones, speaking an almost preconceived essay of commentary or artificial sentimentality.

to become king (Act One Scene 4, modern line numbering 22–27). Ff show a Macbeth almost swamped with extra thoughts as he assures Duncan

> The service,* and the loyaltie I owe,
> In doing it,* payes it selfe.
> Your highnesse part,* is to receive our Duties,
> And our Duties are to your Throne,* and State,
> Children,* and Servants; which doe but what they should,*
> By doing every thing safe toward your Love
> And Honour.

The heavy use of minor punctuation—especially when compared with most modern texts which remove the commas marked *, leaving Macbeth with just six thoughts compared to Ff's twelve—clearly shows a man ill at ease and/or working too hard to say the right thing. Again the punctuation helps create an understanding of the character.

However, while the minor punctuation is extremely important in the discovery process of reading and/or rehearsal, paradoxically, it mustn't become too dominant. From the performance/speaking viewpoint, to pause at each comma would be tantamount to disaster. There would be an enormous dampening effect if reader/actor were to pause at every single piece of punctuation: the poetry would be destroyed and the event would become interminable.

In many ways, minor punctuation is the Victorian child of Shakespearean texts, it must be seen but not heard. (In speaking the text, the new thought the minor punctuation represents can be added without pausing: a change in timbre, rhythm, or pitch—in acting terms, occurring naturally with changes in intention—will do the trick.)

But once thoughts have been discovered, they have to be organised into some form of coherent whole. If the period shows the end of one world and the start of the new, and if the comma marks a series of small, ever-changing, ever-evolving thoughts within each world, occasionally there must be pause for reflection somewhere in the helter-skelter of tumbling new ideas. This is the **major punctuation's** strength; major punctuation consisting of the semicolon [;], and the colon [:].

Major punctuation marks the gathering together of a series of small thoughts within an overall idea before moving onto something new. If a room full of Rodin sculptures were analogous to an Elizabethan scene or act, each individual piece of sculpture would be a speech, the torso or back or each major limb a separate sentence. Each collective body part (a hand, the wrist, the forearm, the upper arm) would be a series of small thoughts bounded by major punctuation, each smaller item within that part (a finger, a fingernail, a knuckle) a single small thought separated by commas. In describing the sculpture to a friend one might move from the smaller details (the knuckle) to the larger (the hand) to another larger (the wrist) then another (the forearm) and so on to the whole limb. Unless the speaker is emotionally moved by the recollection, some pauses would be essential, certainly after finishing the whole description of the arm (the sentence), and probably after each major collective of the hand, the wrist, etc. (as marked by the major punctuation), but not after every small bit.

As a rule of thumb, and simply stated, the colon and semicolon mark both a thinking and a speaking pause. The vital difference between major and minor punctuation, whether in the silent reading of the text or the performing of it aloud, is you need not pause at the comma, bracket, or dash; you probably should at the colon, semicolon, and period.

Why the Major Punctuation is Bolded in These Texts.

In speaking the text or reading it, the minor punctuation indicates the need to key onto the new thought without necessarily requiring a pause. In so doing, the inherent rhythms of speech, scene, and play can clip along at the rate suggested by the Prologue in *Romeo and Juliet*, 'the two hours traffic of the stage', until a pause is absolutely necessary. Leave the commas alone, and the necessary pauses will make themselves known.

The 'major' punctuation then comes into its own, demanding double attention as both a thinking and speaking device. This is why it is bolded, to highlight it for the reader's easier access. The reader can still use all the punctuation when desired, working through the speech thought by thought, taking into account both major and minor punctuation as normal. Then, when needed, the bolding of the major punctuation will allow the reader easy access for marking where the speech, scene, or play needs to be broken down into its larger thinking/speaking (and even breathing) units without affecting its overall flow.

The Blank Pages Within the Text

In each text within this series, once readers reach the play itself they will find that with each pair of pages the dialogue is printed on the right-hand page only. The left-hand page has been deliberately left blank so that readers, actors, directors, stage managers, teachers, etc. have ample space for whatever notes and text emendations they may wish to add.

PRACTICAL ON-PAGE HELP FOR THE READER

THE VISUAL SYMBOLS HIGHLIGHTING MODERN ALTERATIONS

THE BOX

This surrounds a passage where the modern texts have made whole-scale alterations to the Ff text. Each boxed section will be footnoted, and the changes analysed at the bottom of the page.

THE FOOTNOTES

With many modern texts the footnotes are not easily accessible. Often no indication is given within the text itself where the problem/choice/correction exists. Readers are forced into a rather cumbersome four-step process. First, they have to search through the bottom of the page where the footnotes are crammed together, often in very small print, to find a line number where an alteration has been made. Then they must read the note to find out what has been altered. Then they must go back to the text and search the side of the page to find the corresponding line number. Having done all this, finally they can search the line to find the word or phrase that has been changed (sometimes complicated by the fact the word in question is set twice in different parts of the line).

These texts will provide a reference marker within the text itself, directly alongside the word or phrase that is in question. This guides the reader directly to the corresponding number in the footnote section of the bottom of each page, to the alteration under discussion — hopefully a much quicker and more immediate process.

In addition, since there are anywhere between 300 and 1,100 footnotes in any one of these texts, a tool is offered to help the reader find only those notes they require, when they require them. In the footnote section, prior to the number that matches the footnote marker in the text, a letter or combination of letters will be set as a code. The letter 'W', for example, shows that the accompanying footnote refers to word substitutions offered by modern texts; the letters 'SD' refer to an added or altered stage direction; the letters 'LS' show the footnote deals with a passage where the modern texts have completely altered the line-structure that F1 set. This enables readers to be selective when they want to examine only certain changes, for they can quickly skim through the body of footnotes until they find the code they want, perhaps those dealing with changes in prefixes (the code 'P') or when modern alterations have been swapping lines from verse to prose or vice versa (the code 'VP'). For full details of the codes, see pp. xxxiii–xxxv below.

Readers are urged to make full use of the footnotes in any of the Recommended Texts listed just before the start of the play. They are excellent in their areas of expertise. To attempt to rival or paraphrase them would be redundant. Thus the footnotes in these scripts will hardly ever deal with word meanings and derivations; social or political history; literary derivations and comparisons; or lengthy quotations from scholars or commentators. Such information is readily available in the *Oxford English Dictionary* and from the recommended modern texts.

Generally, the footnotes in these scripts will deal with matters theatrical and textual and will be confined to three major areas: noting where and how the modern texts alter F1's line structure; showing popular alternative word readings often selected by the modern texts (these scripts will keep the F1 reading unless otherwise noted); and showing the rare occasions where and how these scripts deviate from their source texts. When the modern texts offer alternative words and/or phrases to F2-4 / Qq, the original spelling and punctuation will be used. Where appropriate, the footnotes will briefly refer to the excellent research of the scholars of the last three centuries, and to possible theatrical reasons for maintaining F1's structural 'irregularities'.

THE SYMBOL °

This will be used to show where modern texts have altered F1's line structure, and will allow the reader to explore both the F1 setting and the modern alternative while examining the speech where it is set, in its proper context and rightful position within the play. For example, though F1 is usually the source text for *Henry the Fifth* and sets the dialogue for Pistoll in prose, most modern texts use the memorial Q version and change his lines to (at times extraordinarily peculiar) verse. These texts will set the speech as shown in F1, but add the ° to show the modern texts alterations, thus:

> Pistoll   Fortune is Bardolphs foe, and frownes on him:°
> for he hath stolne a Pax, and hanged must a be:° a damned
> death:° let Gallowes gape for Dogge, let Man goe free,°
> and let not Hempe his Wind-pipe suffocate:° but Exeter
> hath given the doome of death,° for Pax of little price.°
>
> Therefore goe speake,° the Duke will heare thy voyce;°
> and let not Bardolphs vitall thred bee cut° with edge of
> Penny-Cord, and vile reproach.°
>   Speake Captaine for
> his Life, and I will thee requite.°
>   (*Henry V*, These Scripts, 2.1.450–459)

Read the speech utilising the ° to mark the end of a line, and the reader is exploring what the modern texts suggest should be the structure. Read the lines ignoring the ° and the reader is exploring what the F1 text really is. Thus both F1 and modern/Q versions can be read within the body of the text.

THE VERTICAL LINE TO THE LEFT OF THE TEXT

This will be used to mark a passage where modern editors have altered F1's verse to prose or vice versa. Here is a passage in a predominantly prose scene from *Henry V*. Modern texts and F1 agree that Williams and Fluellen should be set in prose. However, the F1 setting for Henry could be in verse, though most modern texts set it in prose too. The thin vertical line to the left of the text is a quick reminder to the reader of disagreement between Ff and modern texts (the F1 setting will always be shown, and the disputed section will be footnoted accordingly).

> King Henry Twas I indeed thou promised'st to strike,
> And thou hast given me most bitter termes.
>
> Fluellen And please your Majestie, let his Neck answere
> for it, if there is any Marshall Law in the World.
>
> King Henry How canst thou make me satisfaction?
>
> Williams All offences, my Lord, come from the heart: ne-
> ver came any from mine, that might offend your Ma-
> jestie. (*Henry V,* These Scripts, 4.1.240–247)

THE SYMBOL } SET TO THE RIGHT OF TEXT, CONNECTING TWO SPEECHES

This will be used to remind readers of the presence of what most modern texts consider to be split or shared lines, and that therefore the second speech could springboard quickly off the first, thus increasing the speed of the dialogue and debate; for example:

> Angelo Did I not tell thee yea? hadst thou not order?
> Why do'st thou aske againe?
> }
> Provost Lest I might be too rash:
> Under your good correction, I have seene
> When after execution . . .

Since there is no definitive way of determining whether Shakespeare wished the two short lines to be used as a shared or split line, or used as two separate short lines, the reader would do well to explore the moment twice. The first time the second speech could be 'springboarded' off the first as if it were a definite shared line; the second time round a tiny break could be inserted before speaking the second speech, as if a hesitation were deliberately intended. This way both possibilities of the text can be examined.

THE SYMBOL → TO THE RIGHT OF THE TEXT, JOINING TWO SHORT LINES
SPOKEN BY A SINGLE CHARACTER

This indicates that though Ff has set two short lines for a single character, perhaps hinting at a minute break between the two thoughts, most modern texts have set the two short lines as one longer one. Thus the first two lines of Juliet's

> How cam'st thou hither. →

> Tell me, and wherefore?
> The Orchard walls are high, and hard to climbe

can be explored as one complete line (the interpretation of most modern texts), or, as F1 suggests, as two separate thoughts with a tiny hesitation between them. In most cases these lines will be footnoted, and possible reasons for the F1 interpretation explored.

THE OCCASIONAL USE OF THE [†]

This marks where F1 has been forced, in a crowded line, to set the end of the line immediately above or below the first line, flush to the right hand column. These texts will set the original as one complete line—the only instance where these scripts do not faithfully reproduce F1's line structure.

THE OCCASIONAL USE OF THE [†] TOGETHER WITH A FOOTNOTE (ALSO SEE P. XXXVII)

This marks where a presumed F1 compositorial mistake has led to a meaningless word being set (for example 'speeh' instead of 'speech') and, since there is a 'correct' form of the word offered by either F2–4 or Qq, the correct form of the word rather than the F1 error has been set. The footnote directs the reader to the original F1 setting reproduced at the bottom of the page.

PATTERNED BRACKETS { } SURROUNDING A PREFIX OR PART OF A STAGE DIRECTION

These will be used on the infrequent occasions where a minor alteration or addition has been made to the original F1 setting.

THE VARIED USE OF THE * AND ∞

This will change from text to text. Sometimes (as in *Hamlet*) an * will be used to show where, because of the 1606 Acte To Restraine The Abuses of Players, F1 had to alter Qq's 'God' to 'Heaven'. In other plays it may be used to show the substitution of the archaic 'a' for 'he' while in others the * and /or the ∞ may be used to denote a line from Qq or F2–4 which F1 omits.

THE SYMBOL •

This is a reminder that a character with several prefixes has returned to one previously used in the play.

THE VISUAL SYMBOLS HIGHLIGHTING KEY ITEMS WITHIN THE FIRST FOLIO

THE DROPPING OF THE TEXT A SINGLE LINE

This indicates where one sentence ends, and a new one begins (see pp. xvii– xviii).

THE BOLDING OF PUNCTUATION

This indicates the presence of the major punctuation (see pp. xviii–xxi).

UNBRACKETED STAGE DIRECTIONS

These are the ones presumed to come from the manuscript copy closest to Shakespeare's own hand (F1 sets them centred, on a separate line). They usually have a direct effect on the scene, altering what has been taking place immediately prior to its setting (see p. ix).

BRACKETED STAGE DIRECTIONS

These are the ones presumed to have been added by the Playhouse. (F1 sets them alongside the dialogue, flush to the right of the column.) They usually support, rather than alter, the onstage action (see p. ix).

(The visual difference in the two sets of directions can quickly point the reader to an unexpected aspect of an entry or exit. Occasionally an entry is set alongside the text, rather than on a separate line. This might suggest the character enters not wishing to draw attention to itself, for example, towards the end of *Macbeth,* the servant entering with the dreadful news of the moving Byrnane Wood. Again, F1 occasionally sets an exit on a separate line, perhaps stopping the onstage action altogether, as with the triumphal exit to a 'Gossips feast' at the end of *The Comedy of Errors* made by most of the reunited and/or business pacified characters, leaving the servant Dromio twins onstage to finish off the play. A footnote will be added when these unusual variations in F1's directions occur.)

As with all current texts, the final period of any bracketed or unbracketed stage direction will not be set.

ACT, SCENE, AND LINE NUMBERING SPECIFIC TO THIS TEXT

Each of these scripts will show the act and scene division from F1. They will also indicate modern act and scene division, which often differs from Ff/Qq. Modern texts suggest that in many plays full scene division was not attempted until the eighteenth century, and act division in the early texts was sometimes haphazard at best. Thus many modern texts place the act division at a point other than that set in Ff/Qq, and nearly always break Ff/Qq text up into extra scenes. When modern texts add an act or scene division which is not shared by F1, the addition will be shown in brackets within the body of each individual play as it occurs. When Ff set a new Act or scene, for clarity these texts will start a fresh page, even though this is not Ff/Qq practice

ON THE LEFT HAND SIDE OF EACH PAGE

Down the left of each page, line numbers are shown in increments of five. These refer to the lines in this text only. Where F1 prints a line containing two sentences, since these scripts set two separate lines, each line will be numbered independently.

On The Top Right Of Each Page

These numbers represent the first and last lines set on the page, and so summarise the information set down the left hand side of the text.

At The Bottom Right Of Each Page: using these scripts with other texts

At times a reader may want to compare these texts with either the original First Folio, or a reputable modern text, or both. Specially devised line numbers will make this a fairly easy proposition. These new reference numbers will be found at the bottom right of the page, just above the footnote section.

The information before the colon allows the reader to compare these texts against any photographic reproduction of the First Folio. The information after the colon allows the reader to compare these texts with a modern text, specifically the excellent *Riverside Shakespeare*.[7]

Before the colon: any photostat of the First Folio

A capital letter plus a set of numbers will be shown followed by a lowercase letter. The numbers refer the reader to a particular page within the First Folio; the capital letter before the numbers specifies whether the reader should be looking at the right hand column (R) or left hand column (L) on that particular page; the lower case letter after the numbers indicates which compositor (mainly 'a' through 'e') set that particular column. An occasional asterisk alongside the reference tells the reader that though this is the page number as set in F1, it is in fact numbered out of sequence, and care is needed to ensure, say in *Cymbeline,* the appropriate one of two 'p. 389s' is being consulted.

Since the First Folio was printed in three separate sections (the first containing the Comedies, the second the Histories, and the third the Tragedies),[8] the pages and section in which each of these scripts is to be found will be mentioned in the introduction accompanying each play. The page number refers to that printed at the top of the reproduced Folio page, and not to the number that appears at the bottom of the page of the book which contains the reproduction.

Thus, from this series of texts, page one of *Measure for Measure* shows the ref-

---

[7] Gwynne Blakemore Evans, Harry Levin, Anne Barton, Herschel Baker, Frank Kermode, Hallet D. Smith, and Marie Edel, eds., *The Riverside Shakespeare* (Copyright © 1974 by Houghton Mifflin Company). This work is chosen for its exemplary scholarship, editing principles, and footnotes.

[8] The plays known as Romances were not printed as a separate section: *Cymbeline* was set with the Tragedies, *The Winter's Tale* and *The Tempest* were set within the Comedies, and though *Pericles* had been set in Q it did not appear in the compendium until F3. *Troilus and Cressida* was not assigned to any section, but was inserted between the Histories and the Tragedies with only 2 of its 28 pages numbered.

erence 'L61–c'. This tells the reader that the text was set by compositor 'c' and can be checked against the left hand column of p. 61 of the First Folio (*Measure For Measure* being set in the Comedy Section of F1).

Occasionally the first part of the reference seen at the bottom of the page will also be seen within the text, somewhere on the right hand side of the page. This shows the reader exactly where this column has ended and the new one begins.

(As any photostat of the First Folio clearly shows, there are often sixty-five lines or more per column, sometimes crowded very close together. The late Professor Charlton Hinman employed a brilliantly simple line-numbering system (known as TLN, short for Through Line Numbering System) whereby readers could quickly be directed to any particular line within any column on any page.

The current holders of the rights to the TLN withheld permission for the system to be used in conjunction with this series of Folio Texts.)

After the colon: *The Riverside Shakespeare*

Numbers will be printed indicating the act, scene, and line numbers in *The Riverside Shakespeare,* which contain the information set on the particular page of this script. Again, using the first page of *Measure For Measure*, the reference 1.1.1–21 on page one of these scripts directs the reader to Act One Scene 1 of *The Riverside Shakespeare*; line one in *The Riverside Shakespeare* matches the first line in this text, while the last line of dialogue on page one of this text is to be found in line twenty-one of the *Riverside* version of the play.

COMMON TYPESETTING PECULIARITIES
OF THE FOLIO AND QUARTO TEXTS
(And How These Texts Present Them)

There are a few (to modern eyes) unusual contemporary Elizabethan and early Jacobean printing practices which will be retained in these scripts.

THE ABBREVIATIONS, 'S.', 'L.', 'D.', 'M.'

Ff and Qq use standard printing abbreviations when there is not enough space on a single line to fit in all the words. The most recognisable to modern eyes includes 'S.' for Saint; 'L.' for Lord; 'M.' for Mister (though this can also be short for 'Master', 'Monsieur', and on occasions even 'Mistress'); and 'D.' for Duke. These scripts will set F1 and footnote accordingly.

'Ÿ', 'W', AND ACCENTED FINAL VOWELS

Ff/Qq's two most commonly used abbreviations are not current today, viz.:

ÿ, which is usually shorthand for either 'you'; 'thee'; 'thou'; 'thy'; 'thine'; or 'yours'

w, usually with a ¨ above, shorthand for either 'which'; 'what'; 'when'; or 'where'. Also, in other cases of line overcrowding, the last letter of a relatively unimportant word is omitted, and an accent placed over the preceding vowel as a marker, e.g. 'thä' for 'than'. For all such abbreviations these scripts will set F1 and footnote accordingly.

THE SPECIAL CASE OF THE QUESTION AND EXCLAMATION MARKS
('?' AND '!')

Usage

Elizabethan use of these marks differs somewhat from modern practice. Ff/Qq rarely set an exclamation mark: instead the question mark was used either both as a question mark and as an exclamation point. Thus occasionally the question mark suggests some minor emphasis in the reading.

Sentence Count

When either mark occurs in the middle of a speech, it can be followed by a capitalised or a lowercase word. When the word is lowercase (not capitalised) the sentence continues on without a break. The opposite is not always true: just because the following word is capitalised does not automatically signify the start of a new sentence, though more often than not it does.

Elizabethan rhetorical writing style allowed for words to be capitalised within a sentence, a practice continued by the F1 compositors. Several times in *The Winters Tale,* highly emotional speeches are set full of question marks followed by capitalised words. Each speech could be either one long sentence of ongoing passionate rush, or up to seven shorter sentences attempting to establish self-control.

The final choice belongs to the individual reader, and in cases where such alternatives arise, the passages will be boxed, footnoted, and the various possibilities discussed.

THE ENDING OF SPEECHES WITH NO PUNCTUATION, OR PUNCTUATION OTHER THAN A PERIOD

Quite often F1–2 will not show punctuation at the end of a speech, or sometimes set a colon (:) or a comma (,) instead. Some commentators suggest the setting of anything other than a period was due to compositor carelessness, and that omission occurred either for the same reason, or because the text was so full it came flush to the right hand side of the column and there was no room left for the final punctuation to be set. Thus modern texts nearly always end a speech with the standard period (.), question mark (?), or exclamation mark (!), no matter what F1–2 have set.

However, omission doesn't always occur when a line is full, and F2, though making over sixteen hundred unauthorised typographical corrections of F1 (more than eight hundred of which are accepted by most modern texts), rarely replaces an offending comma or colon with a period, or adds missing periods—F3 is the first to make such alterations on a large scale basis. A few commentators, while acknowledging some of the omissions/mistakes are likely to be due to compositor or scribal error, suggest that ending the speech with anything other than a period (or not ending the speech at all) might indicate that the character with the speech immediately following is in fact interrupting this first speaker.

These texts will set F1, footnote accordingly, and sometimes discuss the possible effect of the missing or 'incorrect' punctuation.

THE SUBSTITUTIONS OF 'i/I' FOR 'j/J' AND 'u' FOR 'v'

In both Ff/Qq words now spelled as 'Jove' or 'Joan' are often set as 'Iove' or 'Ioan'. To avoid confusion, these texts will set the modern version of the word. Similarly, words with 'v' in the middle are often set by Ff/Qq with a 'u'; thus the modern word 'avoid' becomes 'auoid'. Again, these texts will set the modern version of the word, without footnote acknowledgement.

ALTERNATIVE SETTINGS OF A WORD WHERE DIFFERENT SPELLINGS MAINTAIN THE SAME MEANING

Ff/Qq occasionally set, what appears to modern eyes, an archaic spelling of a word for which there is a more common modern alternative, for example 'murther' for murder, 'burthen' for burden, 'moe' for more, 'vilde' for vile. Some modern texts set the Ff/Qq spelling, some modernise. These texts will set the F1 spelling throughout.

ALTERNATIVE SETTINGS OF A WORD WHERE DIFFERENT SPELLINGS SUGGEST DIFFERENT MEANINGS

Far more complicated is the situation where, while an Elizabethan could substitute one word formation for another and still imply the same thing, to modern eyes the substituted word has a entirely different meaning to the one it has replaced. The following is by no means an exclusive list of the more common dual-spelling, dual-meaning words:

anticke–antique	mad–made	sprite–spirit
born–borne	metal–mettle	sun–sonne
hart–heart	mote–moth	travel–travaill
human–humane	pour–(powre)–power	through–thorough
lest–least	reverent–reverend	troth–truth
lose–loose	right–rite	whether–whither

Some of these doubles offer a metrical problem too; for example 'sprite', a one syllable word, versus 'spirit'. A potential problem occurs in *A Midsummer Nights Dream*, where provided the modern texts set Q1's 'thorough', the scansion pattern of elegant magic can be established, whereas F1's more plebeian 'through' sets up a much more awkward and clumsy moment.

These texts will set the F1 reading, and footnote where the modern texts' substitution of a different word formation has the potential to alter the meaning (and sometimes scansion) of the line.

'THEN' AND 'THAN'

These two words, though their neutral vowels sound different to modern ears, were almost identical to Elizabethan speakers and readers, despite their different meanings. Ff and Qq make little distinction between them, setting them interchangeably. In these scripts the original printings will be used, and the modern reader should soon get used to substituting one for the other as necessary.

'I', AND 'AY'

Ff/Qq often print the personal pronoun 'I' and the word of agreement 'aye' simply as 'I'. Again, the modern reader should quickly get used to this and make the substitution whenever necessary. The reader should also be aware that very occasionally either word could be used and the phrase make perfect sense, even though different meanings would be implied.

'MY SELFE/HIM SELFE/HER SELFE' VERSUS 'MYSELF/HIMSELF/ HERSELF'

Generally Ff/Qq separate the two parts of the word, 'my selfe' while most modern texts set the single word 'myself'. The difference is vital, based on Elizabethan philosophy. Elizabethans regarded themselves as composed of two parts, the corporeal 'I', and the more spiritual part, the 'selfe'. Thus when an Elizabethan character refers to 'my selfe', he or she is often referring to what is to all intents and purposes a separate being, even if that being is a particular part of him- or herself. Thus soliloquies can be thought of as a debate between the 'I' and 'my selfe', and in such speeches, even though there may be only one character onstage, it's as if there were two distinct entities present.

These texts will show F1 as set.

FOOTNOTE CODE
(shown in two forms, the first alphabetical,
the second grouping the codes by topic)

To help the reader focus on a particular topic or research aspect, a special code has been developed for these texts. Each footnote within the footnote section at the bottom of each page of text has a single letter or series of letters placed in front of it guiding readers to one specific topic; thus 'SPD' will direct readers to footnotes just dealing with songs, poems, and doggerel.

ALPHABETICAL FOOTNOTE CODING

A	asides
AB	abbreviation
ADD	a passage modern texts have added to their texts from F2–4/Qq
ALT	a passage (including act and scene division) that has been altered by modern texts without any Ff/Qq authority
COMP	a setting probably influenced by compositor interference
F	concerning disputed facts within the play
FL	foreign language
L	letter or letters
LS	alterations in line structure
M	Shakespeare's use of the scansion of magic (trochaic and seven syllables)
N	a name modern texts have changed or corrected for easier recognition
O	F1 words or phrases substituted for a Qq oath or blasphemy
OM	passage, line, or word modern texts omit or suggest omitting
P	change in prefix assigned to a character
PCT	alterations to F1's punctuation by modern and/or contemporary texts
Q	material rejected or markedly altered by Qq not usually set by modern texts
QO	oaths or blasphemies set in Qq not usually set by modern texts
SD	stage directions added or altered by modern texts
SP	a solo split line for a single character (see pp. xv–xvi above)

SPD	matters concerning songs, poems, or doggerel
?ST	where, because of question marks within the passage, the final choice as to the number of sentences is left to the reader's discretion
STRUCT	a deliberate change from the F1 setting by these texts
UE	an unusual entrance (set to the side of the text) or exit (set on a separate line)
VP	F1's verse altered to prose or vice versa, or lines indistinguishable as either
W	F1's word or phrase altered by modern texts
WHO	(in a convoluted passage) who is speaking to whom
WS	F1 line structure altered because of casting off problems (see pp. x–xi above)

FOOTNOTE CODING BY TOPIC

STAGE DIRECTIONS, ETC.

A	asides
P	change in prefix assigned to a character
SD	stage directions added or altered by modern texts
UE	an unusual entrance (set to the side of the text) or exit (set on a separate line)
WHO	(in a convoluted passage) who is speaking to whom

LINE STRUCTURE AND PUNCTUATION, ETC.

L	letter or letters
LS	alterations in line structure
M	Shakespeare's use of the scansion of magic (trochaic and seven syllables)
PCT	alterations to F1's punctuation by modern and/or contemporary texts
SPD	matters concerning songs, poems, or doggerel
?ST	where, because of question marks within the passage, the final choice as to the number of sentences is left to the reader's discretion
SP	a solo split line for a single character (see pp. xv–xvi above)
VP	F1's verse altered to prose or vice versa, or lines indistinguishable as either

WS	F1 line structure altered because of casting off problems (see pp. x–xi above)

CHANGES TO WORDS AND PHRASES

AB	abbreviation
F	concerning disputed facts within the play
FL	foreign language
N	a name modern texts have changed or corrected for easier recognition
O	F1 words or phrases substituted for a Qq oath or blasphemy
QO	oaths or blasphemies set in Qq not usually set by modern texts
W	F1's word or phrase altered by modern texts

CHANGES ON A LARGER SCALE AND OTHER UNAUTHORISED CHANGES

ADD	a passage modern texts have added to their texts from F2–4/Qq
ALT	a passage (including act and scene division) that has been altered by modern texts without any Ff/Qq authority
COMP	a setting probably influenced by compositor interference
OM	passage, line, or word modern texts omit or suggest omitting
Q	material rejected or markedly altered by Qq not usually set by modern texts
STRUCT	a deliberate change from the F1 setting by these texts

ONE MODERN CHANGE FREQUENTLY NOTED IN THESE TEXTS

'MINUTE' CHANGES TO THE SYLLABLE LENGTH OF FF LINES

As noted above on pages xi–xii, modern texts frequently correct what commentators consider to be large scale metric deficiencies, often to the detriment of character and scene. There are many smaller changes made too, especially when lines are either longer or shorter than the norm of pentameter by 'only' one or two syllables. These changes are equally troublesome, for there is a highly practical theatrical rule of thumb guideline to such irregularities, viz.:

> if lines are slightly **longer** than pentameter, then the characters so involved have too much information coursing through them to be contained within the 'norms' of proper verse, occasionally even to the point of losing self-control

> if lines are slightly **shorter** than ten syllables, then either the information therein contained or the surrounding action is creating a momentary (almost need to breath) hesitation, sometimes suggesting a struggle to maintain self-control

These texts will note all such alterations, usually offering the different syllable counts per line as set both by F1 and by the altered modern texts, often with a brief suggestion as to how the original structural 'irregularity' might reflect onstage action.

FINALLY, A BRIEF WORD ABOUT THE COMPOSITORS [9]

Concentrated research into the number of the compositors and their habits began in the 1950s and, for a while, it was thought five men set the First Folio, each assigned a letter, 'A' through 'E'.

'E' was known to be a seventeen-year-old apprentice whose occasional mishaps both in copying text and securing the type to the frame have led to more than a few dreadful lapses, notably in *Romeo and Juliet*, low in the left column on p. 76 of the Tragedies, where in sixteen F1 lines he commits seven purely typographical mistakes. Compositor 'B' set approximately half of F1, and has been accused of being cavalier both with copying text and not setting line ending punctuation when the line is flush to the column edge. He has also been accused of setting most of the so called 'solo' split lines, though a comparison of other compositors' habits suggests they did so too, especially the conglomerate once considered to be the work of a single compositor known as 'A'. It is now acknowledged that the work set by 'A' is probably the work of at least two and more likely five different men, bringing the total number of compositors having worked on F1 to nine ('A' times five, and 'B' through 'E').

It's important to recognise that the work of these men was sometimes flawed. Thus the footnotes in these texts will point the reader to as many examples as possible which current scholarship and research suggest are in error. These errors fall into two basic categories. The first is indisputable, that of pure typographical mistakes ('wh?ch' for 'which'): the second, frequently open to challenge, is failure to copy exactly the text (Qq or manuscript) which F1 has used as its source material.

As for the first, these texts place the symbol † before a footnote marker within the text (not in the footnote section), a combination used only to point to a purely typographical mistake. Thus in the error-riddled section of *Romeo and Juliet* quoted above, p. 109 of this script shows fourteen footnote markers, seven of them coupled with the symbol †. Singling out these typographical-only markers alerts the reader to compositor error, and that (usually) the 'correct' word or phrase has been set within the text. Thus the reader doesn't have to bother with the footnote below unless they have a morbid curiosity to find out what the error actually is. Also, by definition, the more † appearing in a passage, the worse set that passage is.

As to the second series of (sometimes challengeable) errors labelled poor copy work, the footnotes will alert the reader to the alternative Qq word or phrase usage preferred by most modern texts, often discussing the alternatives in detail, especially when there seems to be validity to the F1 setting.

---

[9] Readers are directed to the ground breaking work of Alice Walker, and also to the ongoing researches of Paul Werstine and Peter W. M. Blayney.

Given the fluid state of current research, more discoveries are bound to be published as to which compositor set which F1 column long after these texts go to print. Thus the current assignation of compositors at the bottom of each of these scripts' pages represents what is known at this moment, and will be open to reassessment as time goes by.

A CAVEAT: THE COMPOSITORS AND 'SINGLE SPLIT LINES' (SEE PP. XV–XVI)

Many commentators suggest single split lines are not Shakespearean dramatic necessity, but compositorial invention to get out of a typesetting dilemma. Their argument is threefold:

first, as mentioned on pp. x–xi, because of 'white space' a small amount of text would have to be artificially expanded to fill a large volume of what would otherwise be empty space: therefore, even though the column width could easily accommodate regular verse lines, the line or lines would be split in two to fill an otherwise embarrassing gap

second, even though the source documents the compositors were using to set F1 showed material as a single line of verse, occasionally there was too much text for the F1 column to contain it as that one single line: hence the line had to be split in two

third, the device was essentially used by compositor B.

There is no doubt that sometimes single split lines did occur for typesetting reasons, but it should be noted that:

single split lines are frequently set well away from white space problems

often the 'too-much-text-for-the-F1-column-width' problem is solved by setting the last one or two words of the overly lengthy line either as a new line, or as an overflow or underflow just above the end of the existing line without resorting to the single split line

all compositors seem to employ the device, especially the conglomerate known as 'A' and compositor E.

As regards the following text, while at times readers will be alerted to the fact that typographical problems could have had an influence on the F1 setting, when single split lines occur their dramatic potential will be discussed, and readers are invited to explore and accept or reject the setting accordingly.

INTRODUCTION TO THE TEXT OF
TWELFE NIGHT, OR WHAT YOU WILL [1]
pages 255 - 275 of the Comedy Section [2]

All Act, Scene, and line numbers will refer to the
Applause text below unless otherwise stated.

Current research places the play as number twenty-two or twenty-three in the canon.
It was set in tandem with *All's Well, That Ends Well* after the completion of *The life and
death of King John* and three pages of *The life and death of King Richard the Second*.

Topical references, especially to the 'Sophy' (a fabled treasure ship) and to the 'new
Mappe with the augmentation of the Indies', suggest the play could not be written any earlier than 1599, when such a map, drawn by Molyneux, was published and Sir Robert
Shirley's ship returned from Persia. John Manningham's diary describes a performance of
Twelve Night at the Middle Temple on February 2nd 1602, a date some scholars contend
was the first performance, despite Leslie Hotson's popular and long-held theory that the
unidentified play performed on January 6th 1602 (the Feast of Epiphany or Twelfth Night)
in front of Don Virginio Orsino, a Tuscan Duke, was in fact Shakespeare's *Twelfe Night*. [3]
Thus the date of composition is commonly accepted as 1601, with Malvolio said to be a por-
trait of Sir William Knollys, (the Queene's comptroller who like Malvolio, had 'sympathy for
Puritanism and a habit of interrupting revelers in his nightshirt' [4]).

SCHOLARS' ASSESSMENT

F1 is the sole authority, and while mid-twentieth century scholars considered
the play to be based on a prompt book [5], current thought is it comes from a somewhat literary transcript (i.e. one made by a professional copyist, hired either

---

[1] For a detailed examination, see Wells, Stanley and Taylor, Gary (eds.). *William Shakespeare: A Textual
Companion.* Oxford: Clarendon Press. 1987. pages 421 - 423: for a detailed analysis of the play's con-
tents, see any of the Recommended Modern Texts.

[2] *Mr. William Shakespeare's Comedies, Histories, & Tragedies, 1623*

[3] Hotson, Leslie: *The First Night of Twelfth Night.* New York: The Macmillan Company. 1954.

[4] Campbell, Oscar James and Edward G. Quinn (eds.). *The Reader's Encyclopedia Of Shakespeare.* New
York: Thomas Y. Crowell. 1966. page 496

[5] A manuscript prepared by the Playhouse (copied from either fair or foul papers) with detailed information
added necessary for staging a theatrical performance. 'Foul papers' is the term used for Shakespeare's
first draft, with all the original crossings out and blots intact.

by Shakespeare or the Playhouse, and probably not a person directly associated with the-atre practice) of Shakespeare's foul papers. [6]

THE TEXT

was set entirely by the reputedly cavalier compositor B. Nevertheless *The New Cambridge Shakespeare Twelfth Night* [7] posits

> the text is remarkably free of verbal cruxes though there are some misprints
> or, perhaps, misreadings, some probable misalignment of speeches, some
> missing stage directions (page 152)

Indeed, the normally metrically precise *A Textual Companion* lists only just over twen-ty passages involving over sixty lines that needed to be altered for *The Oxford Shakespeares* [8], the largest proportion of which deal with the settings of one song (page 39) and one chant (page 84).

BLAMING COMPOSITOR B

There is evidence of one of his foibles with the occasional lack of a period to end some speeches (though many of them have a wonderful theatrical impact as discussed below). There are obvious incorrect mixtures of letters in his tray (c/e, t/r, t/l), leading him to set the peculiar 'sttong' instead of 'strong' as one example of several, (page 3, line 1.1.14). There is also the continuation of the upper-case/lower-case 'y' substitution where several what appear to be verse lines starting with the letter 'y' are set with a lower-case 'y' instead of the expected upper-case letter 'Y'. [9]

But in the search for modern text tidiness, there are possibly some unnecessary or damaging 'corrections'.

• NORMALISING HUMAN FRAILTIES BY REGULARISING PUNCTUATION

In general, the bulk of F1's punctuation escapes without comment, except for an occa-sional reference to an unusual number of colons. However, F1's ungrammatical punctua-tion (which is usually changed) often gives rise to theatrical treasure.

---

[6] *A Textual Companion* suggests F1 setting of "Finis, Actus primus" is 'virtually conclusive evidence for some sort of literary transcript' (page 421).

[7] Donno, E. S. (ed.). *Twelfth Night. The New Cambridge Shakespeare.* Cambridge: Cambridge University Press. 1985

[8] Wells, Stanley and Taylor, Gary (eds.). *The Oxford Shakespeare, William Shakespeare, The Complete Works, Original Spelling Edition/Modern Spelling Edition.* Oxford: The Clarendon Press. 1986

[9] See footnotes #2 and #3, page 55 for examples, and #7, page 53 for a fuller explanation. While most mod-ern texts set an upper-case 'Y' throughout, it may be well worthwhile exploring the examples on pages 53 and 55 as possible momentary slips from the verse formality of what is obviously an awkward situation for both Olivia and Viola.

There is **the classic** (not to say dreadful) **alteration for Sir Toby Belch**, where his F1 recognition of himself as great a fool as Andrew

> Toby   Will you helpe an Asse-head, and a coxcombe, &
>   a knave: a thin fac'd knave, a gull ?
>
> (page 94, lines 5. 1. 219 - 20)

is totally changed to a vicious attack on Andrew simply by the unnecessary modern addition of punctuation, usually a question mark

> Toby   Will you helpe ? - an Asse-head, and a coxcombe, &
>   a knave: a thin fac'd knave, a gull ?

This is one of the most disastrous punctuation alterations in all of Shakespeare.

Similar fiddling alters **the middle of Viola's appalled/amused recognition that Olivia is in love with her**, as F1 sets a jumbled ungrammatical onrush of

> She loves me sure,* the cunning of her passion
> Invites me in this churlish messenger:*
> None of my Lords Ring ?   Why he sent her none;*
> I am the man, if it be so, as tis,
> Poore Lady, she were better love a dreame:*
> Disguise, I see thou art a wickednesse,
> Wherein the pregnant enemie does much.
>
> How easie is it, for the proper false
> In womens waxen hearts to set their formes:*
>
> (pages 28 - 9, lines 2. 2. 24 - 33)

F1 shows an uncertain character in the midst of working matters out where the situation almost runs away with her. Most modern texts set complete rationality by the creation of five new grammatical sentences, marked by the asterisks, thus establishing a woman much more in control.

A similar reworking affects **Olivia at her most vulnerable** where, face to face with Viola/Cesario, and having been told that despite her passionate self-revelations her feelings are not reciprocated, F1 sets

> O what a deale of scorne, lookes beautifull ? *
> In the contempt and anger of his lip,*
> A murdrous guilt shewes not it selfe more soone,
> Then love that would seeme hid: Loves night, is noone.
>
> (page 55, lines 3. 1. 155 - 8)

The two asterisked pieces of punctuation set up Olivia's lack of control. The first establishes a moment of ungrammatical exclamation (one of the functions of the Elizabethan question mark), with the second providing an emotional onrush via the comma. Modern texts' grammatical reworking establishes control instead

> O what a deale of scorne lookes beautifull *
> In the contempt and anger of his lip? *

> A murdrous guilt shewes not it selfe more soone,
> Then love that would seeme hid: Loves night, is noone.

The lack of periods at the end of speeches can really add a kick to the action, as with the opening of Act Two Scene 3 where the colon at the end of the very first line, in which Andrew attempts to leave

> No faith, Ile not stay a jot longer:*

(page 57, line 3 . 2. 1)

allows Toby to interrupt with the calming 'Thy reason deere venom, give thy reason.' This applies equally to the love-lorne Orsino's interruption of Viola/Cesario's reply to a rather personal yet public comment by Olivia

{Olivia}	Cesario, you do not keepe promise with me.
Viola	Madam:*
Orsino	Gracious Olivia

(page 90, lines 5. 1. 106 - 8)

A complete lack of punctuation marks Viola's attempt to swap wits with Feste (page 50, lines 6 - 7, his speech ending 'my house dooth stand by the Church*'). Similarly, F1's lack of punctuation in the <u>middle</u> of a speech (where modern texts add a period) allows Sebastian's youthful exuberance full rein as he pleads with Anthonio not to go to their lodgings but to see the 'memorials, and things of fame/That do renowne this City'

> I am not weary, and 'tis long to night *
> I pray you let us satisfie our eyes

(page 60, lines 3. 3. 23 - 4)

In all of the above examples, modern texts replace the F1 asterisked (lack of) punctuation with periods.

● A DRUNKEN ANDREW, OR A COMPOSITOR'S MISTAKE ?

At times the setting of the **words** offers interesting possibilities. Much has been made of the end of the first scene between Toby and Andrew, where, following the disastrous layout of the bottom of F1 column R 256 (this text page 11, lines 1. 3. 142 - 151), editors argue B has been equally sloppy at the top of the next page. The text involved is set as

Andrew	I, 'tis strong, and it does indifferent well in a dam'd* colour'd stocke. Shall we sit* about some Revels ?
Toby	What shall we do else: were we not borne under Taurus ?
Andrew	Taurus ? That* sides and heart.
Toby	No sir, it is leggs and thighes:let me see thee caper. Ha, higher:ha, ha, excellent.

The three asterisked words have all been reset, 'dun' - a muddy colour - for 'dam'd'; 'set' for 'sit' and 'That's' for 'That'. The replacements are grammatically and typographically correct, yet taken in conjunction with Andrew's propensity for drink, the words as set might just give a clue that Andrew is slightly tipsy, especially given his current actions in the scene, culminating in Toby's enticing him into dancing off-stage.

F1'S STAGE MANAGEMENT OF THE PLAY

Prefixes present little problem, except for those few described below. The stage directions follow F1's usual pattern of rarely setting anything that is apparent from the dialogue. Entries are usually sufficiently detailed for the principal characters though sometimes a little cavalier with the smaller roles, and occasionally an exit is incomplete, as noted below or in the footnotes of the play text.

PREFIXES

- **SOMETIMES THOSE USED DO NOT MATCH THE NAMES OR TITLES SPOKEN IN THE DIALOGUE**

Though **Orsino's** prefix throughout is Duke, he is only so named four times in the dialogue, all in Act One. For the rest of the play he is referred by the lesser title 'Count' no fewer than twelve times [10] plus one highly vulgar approximation spoken by his rival in love, Aguecheeke. [11]

Olivia is referred to by her prefix throughout, though the stage direction for her first entry describes her as 'Lady' Olivia.

- **THE PROBLEMS OF DISGUISE**

As in all Qq/Ff texts, once a character has disguised itself, it is very rarely that a stage direction or entry will draw any further attention to it. The theatre people for whom the texts were originally intended were hardly likely to forget the chance to wear a new costume. Thus the fact that **Viola** adopts the name 'Cesario' for her disguise as a eunuch is referred to immediately on her first appearance as a man (though her prefix always refers to her true female state, Viola) but never referred to in a stage direction. One stage direction incorrectly names her as Violenta (page 20).

Feste is named as Clowne throughout, and the only time this presents a problem is when he is playing Sir Topaz in the tormenting of Malvolio (pages 82 - 4), in that when he talks to himself as Sir Topaz the shifts in dialogue occur so quickly it is sometimes difficult to tell 'which' Feste is speaking when.

---

[10] Which of course means that Olivia as the daughter of a Count, is on an equal, and not lesser, footing with him.

[11] See footnote #6 to page 9.

- OTHER AWKARDNESSES

As usual F1 sets a series of unspecified supernumeraries - other Lords, Saylors, others, Lords, and Attendants. Also, though prefixes are set for 1st and 2nd Officers, more may be included in the Act Three Scene 4 entry (page 73 this text).

The **sailor who rescues Sebastian** is twice named Antonio in the first scene, and then as Anthonio (8 times) in the later dialogue once they arrive in Illyria.

DIRECTIONS APPARENT FROM THE TEXT

- THE EXCHANGE OF MONEY

This is a play where the giving of money for services rendered is very important, yet none of the following incidents is deemed worthy of a separate F1 note - Olivia offering a purse to Viola as both present and in an effort to get her to return - a gift which is refused (page 24, line 1. 5. 311); Toby and Andrew to Feste for a song (page 31, lines 2. 3. 36 - 9); Orsino to Feste in payment for his song (page 39, line 2. 4. 70); Viola to Feste to get him to announce her to Olivia (page 51, line 2. 5. 44); Anthonio to Sebastian to help him enjoy the town (page 61, lines 3. 3. 43 - 52); Viola sharing half her meagre purse with Anthonio who, believing she is Sebastian, expects full return of his own purse (page 74, lines 3. 4. 368 - 70); Sebastian to Feste to get Feste to leave him alone (Feste believing Sebastian to be Cesario whom he has been sent to seek), page 77, lines 4. 1. 19 - 20; and the two separate coins from Orsino to Feste in part for his jokes and in part to bring Olivia to him (page 88, lines 5. 1. 25 - 46).

- TOBY'S DRUNKENNESS

The fact of Toby's being drunk so early in the day, staggering and belching, is not set since again it is all covered in the dialogue (pages 18 - 19, lines 1. 5. 119 - 144).

- MALVOLIO'S WOOING EXCESSES

Malvolio's adopting all the clothing and mannerisms Olivia cannot stand (smiling, 'his face into more lynes, then is in the new Mappe, with the augmentation of the Indies', cross-gartered and in yellow stockings) is similarly established in nauseating detail by Maria (page 59, lines 3. 2. 79 - 85).

- THE LACK OF 'INNER' STAGE DIRECTIONS

F1, rarely indicates actions <u>within</u> the scene, especially when they are apparent from the workings of the play. Usually they are added by modern texts. This would include the to-ing and fro-ing by Sir Toby and Feste in the attempt to get Andrew and 'Cesario' to fight, the details of the non-fight, and the arrest, seizure and surrender of Anthonio (pages 70 - 4).

- ASIDES AND WHO-TO'S [12]

Though at times plentiful, as in the box tree scene (pages 43 - 7), they present little or no problem, save as mentioned earlier when Feste plays the dual roles of himself and Sir Topaz (pages 82 - 4). Occasionally, however, directions dealing with 'from-what' and 'in what manner' would be desirable, for F1 is not always clear in its layout of the text when Malvolio is reading from the supposed Olivia love letter and when commenting (pages 45 - 8), nor when Toby is singing and when not, especially when taunting Malvolio in the night revels (pages 33 - 4).

ENTRIES AND EXITS NOT SO APPARENT FROM THE TEXT

- DISAPPEARING CHARACTERS

Curio is named with the 'other Lords' in the first entry of the play. Valentine is given a separate entry from his (failed) visit to Olivia, and both are mentioned in separate entries in Orsino's next scene, Act One Scene 4. Yet Valentine is never mentioned again while Curio is shown as accompanying Orsino both in Act Two Scene 4 and Act Five. And in some cases neither entries nor exits are set, as with the Musicians to whom Orsino speaks in Act One Scene 1 and Act Two Scene 4.

- DOES OLIVIA ENTER TOO SOON ?

At least one entry seems to be too early for some modern editors. Thus, though F1's first entry of 'Lady Olivia, with Malvolio' (page 15) comes four and a half lines before Feste acknowledges her, most modern texts advance it to just before his greeting. However, as set in F1, Feste may have drawn himself to one side of the stage out of her sight in order to get himself together before daring to come into her angry (with him) presence.

- EXITS OFTEN NOT SET WHEN THEY ARE REFERRED TO IN THE DIALOGUE

This includes Olivia's command to her Gentlewoman, Toby and Andrew,

> Let the Garden doore be shut, and leave mee to
> my hearing.
>
> (page 53, lines 3. 1. 95 - 6)

and some exits are not set even when the text is very obscure to modern eyes, as with Toby's response to being told that Olivia and Cesario are coming

> I wil meditate the while upon some horrid message
> for a Challenge.
>
> (page 69, lines 3. 4. 215 - 6)

---

12 Asides are lines spoken by one character either directly to the audience, or to a small sub-group within a larger group on-stage, and not meant to be heard by anyone else. 'Who-to's are suggestions as to which particular on-stage character out of a larger-group is being addressed by a particular remark. Both are usually modern text additions: Q/F rarely set such indications.

- **INCOMPLETE EXITS**

This occurs in the first scene at Olivia's, for there is no indication when Maria left to be able to return to make the page 17 first announcement of 'there is at the gate, a young Gentleman, much desires to speake with you?' And when does the Clowne leave to look after Toby - before, during or after Malvolio's page 19 entry?

And talking of Feste, once Malvolio arrives to break up the night's revels when does Feste leave? It seems that he doesn't stay till the end since Maria, in plotting her revenge against Malvolio, refers to Toby and Andrew as 'you two', and then as an afterthought refers to the Clowne almost in the absentia 'and let the Foole make a third', page 36, lines 2. 3. 186 - 7.

Then, in the last scene, do the wounded Toby and Andrew stay on-stage to see the resolution of the Sebastian-Viola as Cesario mystery, or do they disappear to get their wounds treated as Olivia orders (page 94, line 5. 4. 221) ? Also, who executes Olivia's command (page 91, line 5.1.150) 'Call forth the holy Father' since the Priest appears unaccompanied eleven lines later? and does the Priest stay till the bitter end? for, once again, no exit is provided for him.

MODERN INTERVENTIONS

THE PERHAPS UNNECESSARY CORRECTIONS OF **F1**'S VERSE AND PROSE

The variations in verse and prose are very few, and small, yet theatrically interesting. Thus, in an admittedly ambiguous setting, F1 shows Olivia twice suddenly moving into a single verse speech in a sea of prose as she toys with Viola

Viola	It alone concernes your eare:I bring no over-ture of warre, no taxation of homage ; I hold the Olyffe in my hand:my words are as full of peace, as matter.	
Olivia *	Yet you began rudely. What are you ?	(9)
	What would you ?	(3)
Viola	The rudenesse that hath appear'd in mee, have I learn'd from my entertainment. What I am, and what I would, are as secret as maiden-head: to your eares, Divinity; to any others, prophanation.	
Olivia *	Give us the place alone,	(6)
	We will heare this divinitie. Now sir, what is your text ?	(14)
Viola	Most sweet Ladie.	
Olivia	A comfortable doctrine, and much may bee saide of it. Where lies your Text ?	

(pages 21 - 2, lines 1. 5. 228 - 245)

a calculated attack perhaps to keep everyone off balance. Most modern texts set the whole as prose.

Then there are two (asterisked) moments for Sebastian when, trailed by the persistent Feste, he moves into prose to threaten the Clowne; quite a large shift in style and approach from the verse he uses before and after the exchange

Sebastian*	I prethee vent thy folly some-where else, thou know'st not me.
Clowne	Vent my folly: He has heard that word of some great man, and now applyes it to a foole. Vent my fol-ly: I am affraid this great lubber the World will prove a Cockney: I prethee now ungird thy strangenes, and tell me what I shall vent to my Lady ? Shall I vent to hir that thou art comming ?
Sebastian*	I prethee foolish greeke depart from me, there's money for thee, if you tarry longer, I shall give worse paiment. (page 77, lines 4. 1. 9 - 21)

F1's shift seems a highly economical way to present both his embarrassment and the slip from grace as he attempts to deal with the situation. Most modern texts again set both of Sebastian's speeches in verse.

THE VERY RARE RESTRUCTURING OF WHAT MAY BE BREAKS IN DECORUM (see also 'BLAMING COMPOSITOR B', pages xl - xlii)

Though there are very few **line structure alterations**, what there are could be important. The most notable affects Malvolio's final confrontation with Olivia whom he believes has betrayed him

Enter Malvolio

Duke	* Is this the Madman ?	(5)
Olivia	I my Lord, this same : How now Malvolio ?	(10-11)
Malvolio	* Madam, you have done me wrong,	(7)
	Notorious wrong.	(4-5)
Olivia	* Have I Malvolio? No.	(6-7)

(page 98, lines 5. 1. 352 - 7)

The first asterisked gap allows a shocked moment (because of Malvolio's appearance?) before the question is asked; the second a moment before Malvolio dare trust his voice; the third for Olivia to maintain her composure before replying. Most modern texts wipe all this out by resetting the passage as shared verse,

Duke	Is this the Madman ?	
Olivia	I my Lord, this same	(10)
	How now Malvolio ?	
Malvolio	Madam, you have done me wrong,	(12-13)
	Notorious wrong .	
Olivia	Have I Malvolio ? No.	(10-12)

Similarly, there are hardly any **single split lines**,[13] save for the magnificent moment for Olivia when she realises she has to ask Cesario the very intimate question about his birthright to see if sociologically he is within her reach

You might do much:	(4)
What is your Parentage?	(6)
	(page 24, lines 1. 5. 303 - 4)

Two more perhaps, if the setting is accepted as verse, can be seen in Malvolio's heightened ridiculousness as he appears before Olivia in his yellow stockings and cross garters

{Maria}	Why how doest thou man ?	(5)*
	What is the matter with thee ?	(7)
		(page 63, lines 3. 4. 27 - 8)

and

Malvolio	At your request:	(4)*
	Yes Nightingales answere Dawes.	(7)
		(page 63, lines 3. 4. 40 - 1)

The first asterisk would allow Maria a moment to choke down her laughter before continuing. The second encourages Malvolio to play to the hilt his 'casting off' of his 'humble slough' while he considers Maria's request before deciding in her favour.

THE LACK OF DEBATE

In such a romantically emotional play there are few opportunities for fast debate. Indeed, Spevack [14] finds just fifty **shared split lines**,[15] quite a few of them coming in the arguments between Orsino and 'Cesario' in Act One Scene 4 (pages 12 - 13) and Act Two Scene 4 (pages 38 and 40 - 1); in the argument leading to the disclosure of Olivia's marriage supposedly to Cesario (pages 91 - 2); with the rest scattered throughout the remaining verse, especially the two handed scenes between Anthonio and Sebastian, Olivia and Viola, and Olivia and Sebastian.

---

[13] These are two or more short verse lines, set for a <u>single</u> character, which if placed together (as poets, scholars and commentators suggest), would form a single full line of verse. These lines are rarely reproduced as set by any modern text . See the General Introduction, pages xv - xvi for further discussion.

[14] Spevack, M. *A Complete And Systematic Concordance To The Works Of Shakespeare.* (9 vols.) Hildesheim. Georg Holms. 1968 - 1980

[15] Two or more short verse lines, set for <u>two or more</u> characters, which if placed together (as poets, scholars and commentators suggest), would form a single full line of verse. See the General Introduction, pages xii - xv for further discussion.

THE SONGS

Feste's love song (pages 31 - 2, lines 2.5.45 - 58) is crammed with **magic**, where all but the first two lines are set in the ritual pattern,[16] thus underscoring the yearning of the words - no wonder Toby and Andrew are moved. None of the other set songs display the pattern.

The words of the catch (page 32) are not set in F1. And as *The New Cambridge Shakespeare Twelfth Night* suggests, part of the insults hurled at Malvolio (pages 33 - 4) are taken from a contemporary popular song, see footnote #2, page 33.

FACTS

The 'CATALOGUE' lists the play as *Twelfe=Night, or what you will:* the title above the text is *Twelfe Night, Or what you will,* while the header is *Twelfe Night, or, What you will.* What should be page 265 is incorrectly set as 273, with the same number then repeated in its correct order. There are no catch word variations, but there are two mistakes (R 258 and R 270).

T.J. King [17] suggests there are 2,338 spoken lines and that eight actors can play nine principal roles. Three boys each play a principal female role. Seven men can play six smaller speaking roles and five mutes: three boys are suggested as three mute attendants[18] on Olivia.

F1's Act and Scene Division is usually accepted as is.

Neil Freeman,
Vancouver, B.C.
Canada, 1998

---

[16] The normal pattern of a regular Shakespearean verse line, known as iambic pentameter, is akin to five pairs of human heart beats, with ten syllables being arranged in five pairs of beats, each pair alternating a pattern of a weak stress followed by a strong stress. Whenever magic is used in the Shakespeare plays (notably in *The Tragedie of Macbeth, The Tempest* and A *Midsommer Nights Dreame*) the form of the spoken verse markedly changes with the line altering in two ways. The length is usually reduced from ten to just seven syllables, and the pattern of stresses is completely reversed, as if the heartbeat was being forced either by the circumstances of the scene or by the need of the speaker to completely change direction.

[17] King, T.J. *Casting Shakespeare's Plays.* Cambridge. Cambridge University Press. 1992

[18] This number seems to be a guesstimate, for the only time 'attendants' are listed (in Olivia's final entry, page 90) no numbers are specified.

RECOMMENDED MODERN TEXTS WITH EXCELLENT
SCHOLARLY FOOTNOTES AND RESEARCH

The footnotes in this text are concise, and concentrate either on matters theatrical or choices in word or line structure which distinguish most modern editions and this Folio based text. Items of literary, historical, and linguistic concern have been well researched and are readily available elsewhere. One of the best **research** works in recent years is

Wells, Stanley, and Gary Taylor, eds. *William Shakespeare: A Textual Companion.* Oxford: Clarendon Press, 1987.

In terms of modern **texts,** readers are urged to consult at least one of the following:

Evans, Gwynne Blakemore, Harry Levin, Anne Barton, Herschel Baker, Frank Kermode, Hallet D. Smith, and Marie Edel, eds. *The Riverside Shakespeare.* Copyright © 1974 by Houghton Mifflin Company.

Donno, E. S. (ed.). *Twelfth Night.* The New Cambridge Shakespeare. 1985

---

l

Dramatis Personæ

The Duke of Illyria's Household

ORSINO, the Duke

VALENTINE, a courtier

CURIO, another courtier

FIRST OFFICER

SECOND OFFICER

Musitians

The House of Mourning

Countesse OLIVIA

Sir TOBY Belch
her uncle, brother of her deceased father

MARIA, her Gentlewoman

MALVOLIO, the Countesse's Steward

the CLOWNE, also known as Feste

FABIAN, a servant in the Countesse's employ

a SERVANT

Waiting Gentlewomen

Visitors to Illyria

Sir ANDREW Aguecheeke
a foolish Knight, would be suitor to Olivia

VIOLA
who later adopts the disguise of a eunuch, Cesario

her twin brother, SEBASTIAN

a Sea CAPTAINE, ship-wrecked with Viola

ANT{H}ONIO, the sea-captaine who rescued Sebastian

a PRIEST

Lords   Saylors   Attendants

This Cast List has been specially prepared for this edition, and will not be found in the Facsimile

Twelfe Night, Or what you will

Actus Primus, Scæna Prima

ENTER ORSINO DUKE [1] OF ILLYRIA, CURIO, AND OTHER
LORDS [2]

Duke	Ift Musicke be the food of Love, play on,
	Give me excesse of it : that surfetting,
	The appetite may sicken, and so dye.
	That straine agen, it had a dying fall :
5	O, it came ore my eare, like the sweet sound
	That breathes upon a banke of Violets ;
	Stealing, and giving Odour.
	Enough, no more,
	'Tis not so sweet now, as it was before.
10	O spirit of Love, how quicke and fresh art thou,
	That notwithstanding thy capacitie,
	Receiveth as the Sea.
	Nought enters there,
	Of what validity, and pitch so ere,
15	But falles into abatement, and low price
	Even in a minute ; so full of shapes is fancie,
	That it alone, is high fantasticall.
Curio	Will you go hunt my Lord?
Duke	What Curio?
20 Curio	The Hart.
Duke	Why so I do, the Noblest that I have :
	O when mine eyes did see Olivia first,
	Me thought she purg'd the ayre of pestilence ;
	That instant was I turn'd into a Hart,
25	And my desires like fell and cruell hounds,

N/P 1 though often referred to in the dialogue as 'Count', most stage directions and prefixes name him as 'Duke'

SD 2 most modern texts add to the stage direction either that Orsino is attended by Musicians, or that he enters to the Musicians who (perhaps) stop playing at his entry

Ere since pursue me.
How now what newes from her?

ENTER VALENTINE [1]

Valentine	So please my Lord, I might not be admitted,
	But from her handmaid do returne this answer:
30	The Element it selfe, till seven yeares heate,[2]
	Shall not behold her face at ample view:
	But like a Cloystresse she will vailed walke,
	And water once a day her Chamber round
	With eye-offending brine: all this to season
35	A brothers dead love, which she would keepe fresh
	And lasting, in her sad remembrance.
Duke	O she that hath a heart of that fine frame
	To pay this debt of love but to a brother,
	How will she love, when the rich golden shaft
40	Hath kill'd the flocke of all affections else
	That live in her.
	When Liver, Braine, and Heart,
	These soveraigne thrones, are all supply'd[3] and fill'd
	Her sweete perfections with one selfe[4] king:
45	Away before me, to sweet beds of Flowres,
	Love-thoughts lye rich, when canopy'd with bowres.

[Exeunt]

L 255 - b

[SD][1] most modern texts place this entry before Orsino's last sentence

[W][2] though most modern texts agree with Ff and print this as 'heate', one gloss = 'hence'

[PCT][3] Ff set no punctuation, though for clarity most modern texts add a comma

[W][4] F1 = 'selfe', F2 = 'selfe same', most modern texts = 'selfsame'

Scena Secunda

ENTER VIOLA, A CAPTAINE, AND SAYLORS

Viola	What Country (Friends) is this?
Captaine	This is Illyria Ladie.
Viola	And what should I do in Illyria?
	My brother he is in Elizium,
5		Perchance he is not drown'd : What thinke you saylors?
Captaine	It is perchance that you your selfe were saved.
Viola	O my poore brother, and so perchance may he be.
Captaine	True Madam, and to comfort you with chance,
	Assure your selfe, after our ship did split,
10		When you, and those poore number saved with you,
	Hung on our driving boate : I saw your brother
	Most provident in perill, binde himselfe,
	(Courage and hope both teaching him the practise)
	To a strong†¹ Maste, that liv'd upon the sea :
15		Where like Orion ² on the Dolphines backe,
	I saw him hold acquaintance with the waves,
	So long as I could see.
Viola	For saying so, there's Gold :ˀ
	Mine owne escape unfoldeth to my hope,
20		Whereto thy speech serves for authoritie
	The like of him.
	Know'st thou this Countrey?
Captaine	I Madam well, for I was bred and borne
	Not three houres travaile from this very place. ³
25 Viola	Who governes heere?
Captaine	A noble Duke in nature, as in name.

ᵂ¹ F2 and most modern texts = 'strong', F1 = 'sttong'

ᴺ² most modern texts correct Ff's spelling of the name ('Orion') to 'Arion'

ᴾᶜᵀ³ F1 sets what might be a colon, F4 sets no punctuation - both suggesting the possibility Viola interrupts him: F2 -3 set a question mark (suggesting emphasis rather than a question): most modern texts set a period

Viola	What is his name?	
Captaine	Orsino.	
Viola	Orsino : I have heard my father name him.	
30	He was a Batchellor then.	
Captaine	And so is now, or was so very late :	
	For but a month ago I went from hence,	
	And then 'twas fresh in murmure (as you know	
	What great ones do, the lesse will prattle of,)	
35	That he did seeke the love of faire Olivia.	
Viola	What's shee?	
Captaine	A vertuous maid, the daughter of a Count	
	That dide some twelvemonth since, then leaving her	
	In the protection of his sonne, her brother,	
40	Who shortly also dide : for whose deere love	
	(They say) she hath abjur'd the sight	
	And company [1] of men.	
Viola	O that I serv'd that Lady,	
	And might not be delivered to the world	R 255 - b
45	Till I had made mine owne occasion mellow	
	What my estate is.	
Captaine	That were hard to compasse,	
	Because she will admit no kinde of suite,	
	No, not the Dukes.	
50 **Viola**	There is a faire behaviour in thee Captaine,	
	And though that nature, with a beauteous wall	
	Doth oft close[†2] in pollution : yet of thee	
	I will [3] beleeve thou hast a minde that suites	
	With this thy faire and outward charracter.	
55	I prethee [4] (and Ile pay thee bounteously)	
	Conceale me what I am, and be my ayde,	
	For such disguise as haply shall become	
	The forme of my intent.	

[w1] for the sake of logic some modern texts reverse the order of F's phrase, and set 'company/And sight . . .'

[w2] F1 = 'cl ose', F2/most modern texts = 'close'

[w3] though most modern texts agree with Ff and print this as 'will', some = 'well'

[w4] though most modern texts set Ff's 'prethee', one commentator suggests setting 'pray thee' thus offering the possibility of Viola punning off her next phrase 'pay thee'

Ile serve this Duke,

60   Thou shalt present me as an Eunuch to him,
               It may be worth thy paines: for I can sing,
               And speake to him in many sorts of Musicke,
               That will allow me very worth his service.
               What else may hap, to time I will commit,
65   Onely shape thou thy silence to my wit.

Captaine   Be you his Eunuch, and your Mute Ile bee,
               When my tongue blabs, then let mine eyes not see.

Viola   I thanke thee: Lead me on.

[Exeunt]

Scæna Tertia

ENTER SIR TOBY, AND MARIA

	Sir Toby	What a plague meanes my Neece to take the death of her brother thus? I am sure care's an enemie to life.
5	Maria	By my troth sir Toby, you must come in earlyer a¹ nights : your Cosin, my Lady, takes great exceptions to your ill houres.
	Toby	Why let her except, before excepted.
10	Maria	I, but you must confine your selfe within the modest limits of order.
	Toby	Confine? Ile confine my selfe no finer then I am : these cloathes are good enough to drinke in, and so bee these boots too : and they be not, let them hang them- selves in their owne straps.
15		
	Maria	That quaffing and drinking will undoe you : I heard my Lady talke of it yesterday : and of a foolish knight that you brought in one night here, to be hir woer²
	Toby	Who, Sir Andrew Ague-cheeke?
20	Maria	I he.
	Toby	He's as tall a man as any's in Illyria.
	Maria	What's that to th'purpose?
	Toby	Why he ha's three thousand ducates a yeare.
25	Maria	I, but hee'l have but a yeare in all these ducates : He's a very foole, and a prodigall.

ᵂ ¹ most modern texts = 'o', F1 = 'a'

ᴾᶜᵀ ² F1 shows no punctuation at the end of the line, perhaps suggesting Toby interrupts Maria: F2 and modern texts add a period

Toby	Fie, that you'l say so : he playes o'th Viol-de-gan-[†1] boys, and speaks three or four languages word for word without booke, & hath all the good gifts of nature.	
Maria	He hath indeed, almost [2] naturall : for besides that he's a foole, he's a great quarreller : and but that hee hath the gift of a Coward, to allay the gust he hath in quarrelling, 'tis thought among the prudent, he would quickely have the gift of a grave.	
Toby	By this hand they are scoundrels and substractors that say so of him.	
	Who are they?	
Maria	They that adde moreover, [†3] hee's drunke nightly in your company.	
Toby	With drinking healths to my Neece : Ile drinke to her as long as there is a passage in my throat, & drinke in Illyria : he's a Coward and a Coystrill that will not drinke to my Neece [4] till his braines turne o'th toe, like a parish top.	L 256 - b
	What wench?	
	Castiliano vulgo : for here coms Sir Andrew Agueface.	

ENTER SIR ANDREW

Andrew	Sir Toby Belch.
	How now sir Toby Belch?
Toby	Sweet sir Andrew.
Andrew	Blesse you faire Shrew.
Maria	And you too sir.
Toby	Accost Sir Andrew, accost.
Andrew	What's that?
Toby	My Neeces Chamber-maid.

[W 1] F2 and most modern texts = 'Viol-de-gam', F1 sets the very peculiar = 'Viol-de-ga n-'

[PCT 2] Ff = ', almost', some modern texts omit the leading comma and set 'all, most'

[W 3] F2 and most modern texts = 'moreover', F1 = 'moreour'

[PCT 4] F1 shows a smudge following 'Neece', F2 sets a comma

55	{Maria} [1]	Good Mistris accost,[2] I desire better acquaintance [3]
	Maria	My name is Mary sir.
	Andrew	Good mistris Mary,[4] accost.
	Toby	You mistake knight: Accost, is front her, boord her, woe her, assayle her.
60	Andrew	By my troth I would not undertake her in this company. Is that the meaning of Accost?
	Maria	Far you well Gentlemen. [5]
65	Toby	And thou let part so Sir Andrew, would thou mightest never draw sword agen.
	Andrew	And you part so mistris, I would I might never draw sword agen: Faire Lady, doe you thinke you have fooles in hand?
	Maria	Sir, I have not you by'th hand.
70	Andrew	Marry but you shall have, and heeres my hand.
	Maria	Now sir, thought is free: I pray you bring your hand to'th Buttry barre, and let it drinke.
75	Andrew	Wherefore (sweet-heart?) What's your Meta- phor?
	Maria	It's dry sir.
	Andrew	Why I thinke so: I am not such an asse, but I can keepe my hand dry. But what's your jest?
80	Maria	A dry jest Sir.
	Andrew	Are you full of them?

[P][1] F2 and most modern texts = 'Andrew', thus correcting F1's dramatically incorrect 'Maria'

[W][2] in both this and his next speech, most modern texts capitalise 'accost', thus re-emphasizing that Andrew thinks Maria's surname is 'accost'

[PCT][3] F1 shows no punctuation at the end of the line, perhaps suggesting Maria interrupts Andrew: F2 and most modern texts add a period

[PCT][4] most modern texts remove the comma to improve the delivery of the joke

[SD][5] most modern texts add a stage direction that Maria starts to leave

Twelfe Night, Or what you will

1. 3. 82 - 110

	Maria	I Sir, I have them at my fingers ends : marry now I let go your hand, I am barren.

[Exit Maria]

85	**Toby**	O knight, thou lack'st a cup of Canarie : [1] when did I see thee so put downe?
	Andrew	Never in your life I thinke, unlesse you see Ca- narie put me downe : mee thinkes sometimes I have no more wit then a Christian, or an ordinary man ha's : but I am a great eater of beefe, and I beleeve that does harme
90		to my wit.
	Toby	No question.
	Andrew	And I thought that, I'de forsweare it. Ile ride home to morrow sir Toby.
95	**Toby**	*Pur-quoy* my deere knight?

	Andrew	What is *purquoy*?
		         Do, or not do?
		           I would I had
		bestowed that time in the tongues, that I have in fencing [2]

100		dancing, and beare-bayting : O had I but followed the Arts.
	Toby	Then hadst thou had an excellent head of haire.
	Andrew	Why, would that have mended my haire?
	Toby	Past question, for thou seest it will [†3] not coole my nature[4] †
105	**Andrew**	But it becoms we [5] wel enough, dost not?
	Toby	Excellent, it hangs like flax on a distaffe : & I hope to see a huswife take thee between her legs, & spin it off.
	Andrew	Faith Ile home to morrow sir Toby, your niece wil not be seene, or if she be it's four to one, she'l none of me :
110		the Connt [6] himselfe here hard by, wooes her,[7]

R 256 - b : 1. 3. 78 - 108

[SD1] some modern texts suggest Toby now hands Andrew a cup of wine

[PCT2] F1 - 2 set no punctuation, F3/most modern texts add a comma

[W3] F1 = 'wlll', F2/most modern texts = 'will'

[W4] F1 = 'coole my nature', without any finishing punctuation, most modern texts set 'curle by nature.'

[W5] F1 = 'we', F2 and most modern texts = 'me'

[W6] F2 and most modern texts = 'Count', F1 = 'Connt'

[PCT7] F1 sets a comma, as if Toby interrupts him: F2/most modern texts set a period

Toby	Shee'l none o'th Count, she'l not match above hir degree, neither in estate, yeares, nor wit: I have heard her swear't. [†1]	
	Tut there's life in't man.	R 256 - b
115 **Andrew**	Ile stay a moneth longer.	
	I am a fellow o'th strangest minde i'th world: I delight in Maskes and Revels sometimes[†] altogether.	
Toby	Art thou good at these kicke-chawses Knight?	
120 **Andrew**	As any man in Illyria, whatsoever he be, under the degree of my betters, & yet I will not compare with an old man.	
Toby	What is thy excellence in a galliard, knight?	
Andrew	Faith, I can cut a caper.	
125 **Toby**	And I can cut the Mutton too't.	
Andrew	And I thinke I have the backe-tricke, simply as strong as any man in Illyria.	
Toby	Wherefore are these things hid?	
130	Wherefore have these gifts a Curtaine before 'em?	
	Are they like to take dust, like mistris Mals picture?	
	Why dost thou not goe to Church in a Galliard, and come home in a Carranto?	
135	My verie walke should be a Jigge: I would not so much as make water but in a Sinke-a-pace: [2] What dooest thou meane?	
	Is it a world to hide vertues in?	
	I did thinke by	
140	the excellent constitution of thy legge, it was form'd under the starre of a Galliard.	

R 256 - b / L 257 - b : 1. 3. 109 - 133

[▼1] F1 = 'swear t', F2 = 'swear't'

[▼2] most modern texts set the correct term for the five-step dance, 'cinque-a-pace', F1 sets the more obvious visual reminder of the pun, 'Sinke-a-pace'

	Andrew	I, 'tis strong, and it does indifferent well in a
		dam'd colour'd [1] stocke.

        . Shall we sit [2] about some Revels?

145   **Toby**   What shall we do else: were we not borne under
                Taurus?

    Andrew   Taurus?
                    That [3] sides and heart.

    Toby   No sir, it is leggs and thighes: let me see thee ca-
150   per.
                Ha, higher: ha, ha, excellent.

[Exeunt]

---

[1] most modern texts = 'dun colour'd', Ff = 'dam'd colour'd': this is the first of three verbal corrections that most modern editors feel they must make to Ff within two and a half lines, all relating to Andrew: while the 'mistakes' may have occurred through poor typesetting, there is also the dramatic possibility that, under Toby's influence, Andrew is getting tipsy or drunk (just as Maria has said happens 'nightly', earlier in the scene, lines 37-8)

[2] most modern texts = 'set', Ff = 'sit', (see fn. #1 above)

[3] F3/most modern texts = 'That's', F1 - 2 = 'That', (see fn. #1 above)

Scena Quarta

ENTER VALENTINE, AND VIOLA IN MANS ATTIRE

Valentine	If the Duke continue these favours towards you
	Cesario, you are like to be much advanc'd, he hath known
	you but three dayes, and already you are no stranger.

Viola	You either feare his humour, or my negligence,
	that you call in question the continuance of his love.

5

Is

he inconstant sir, in his favours.   **Valentine**   No beleeve me.

ENTER DUKE, CURIO, AND ATTENDANTS [1]

Viola	I thanke you: heere comes the Count.
Duke	Who saw Cesario hoa?
Viola	On your attendance my Lord heere.

10

Duke	Stand you a-while aloofe. [2]
	Cesario,
	Thou knowst no lesse, but all: I have unclasp'd
	To thee the[†3] booke even of my secret soule.

	Therefore good youth, addresse thy gate unto her,
	Be not deni'de accesse, stand at her doores,[4]
	And tell them, there thy fixed foot shall grow
	Till thou have audience.

15

Viola	Sure my Noble Lord,
	If she be so abandon'd to her sorrow
	As it is spoke, she never will admit me.

20

Duke	Be clamorous, and leape all civill bounds,
	Rather then make unprofited returne,[5]

[SD1] most modern texts delay the entry until after Viola's next line

[SD2] most modern texts add a stage direction for all to withdraw from the Duke and Viola

[W3] F1 = 'rhe', F2/most modern texts = 'the'

[PCT4] F1's punctuation is somewhat blurred, F2/most modern texts set a comma

[PCT5] F2 and most modern texts set a period, F1 alone sets a comma, perhaps suggesting Viola interrupts him

Viola	Say I do speake with her (my Lord) what then?	
25 **Duke**	O then, unfold the passion of my love,	
	Surprize her with discourse of my deere faith ;	
	It shall become thee well to act my woes :	
	She will attend it better in thy youth,	
	Then in a Nuntio's of more grave aspect.	
30 **Viola**	I thinke not so, my Lord.	
Duke	Deere Lad, beleeve it ;	L 257 - b
	For they shall yet belye thy happy yeeres,	
	That say thou art a man : Dianas lip	
	Is not more smooth, and rubious : thy small pipe	
35	Is as the maidens organ, shrill, and sound,	
	And all is semblative a womans part.	
	I know thy constellation is right apt	
	For this affayre : some foure or five attend him,	
	All if you will : for I my selfe am best	
40	When least in companie : prosper well in this,	
	And thou shalt live as freely as thy Lord,	
	To call his fortunes thine.	
Viola	Ile do my best	
	To woe your Lady : [1] yet a barrefull strife,	
45	Who ere I woe, my selfe would be his wife.	

[Exeunt]

L 257 - b / R 257 - b : 1. 4. 23 - 42

---

[1] most modern texts indicate the following is spoken as an aside

Scena Quinta

	Maria	Nay, either tell me where thou hast bin, or I will not open my lippes so wide as a brissle may enter, in way of thy excuse : my Lady will hang thee for thy absence.
5	Clowne	Let her hang me : hee that is well hang'de in this world, needs to feare no colours.
	Maria	Make that good.
	Clowne	He shall see none to feare.
	Maria	A good lenton answer : I can tell thee where ÿ [1] saying was borne, of I feare no colours.
10	Clowne	Where good mistris Mary?
	Maria	In the warrs, & that may you be bolde to say in your foolerie.
	Clowne	Well, God give them wisedome that have it : & those that are fooles, let them use their talents.
15	Maria	Yet you will be hang'd for being so long absent, or to be turn'd away : is not that as good as a hanging to you?
	Clowne	Many a good hanging, prevents a bad marriage : and for turning away, let summer beare it out.
20	Maria	You are resolute then?
	Clowne	Not so neyther, but I am resolv'd on two points [2]
	Maria	That if one breake, the other will hold : or if both breake, your gaskins fall.

[AB] [1] F1 = 'ÿ', (printed as such because of lack of column width), F2/most modern texts = 'that'

[PCT] [2] F1 sets no punctuation, F2 sets a period, most modern texts set a dash, suggesting Maria interrupts him

Clowne		Apt in good faith, very apt: well go thy way, if
25		sir Toby would leave drinking, thou wert as witty a piece
		of Eves flesh, as any in Illyria.
	Maria	Peace you rogue, no more o'that: here comes my
		Lady: make your excuse wisely, you were best. [1]

ENTER LADY OLIVIA, WITH MALVOLIO [2]

	Clowne	Wit, and't be thy will, put me into good fooling:
30		those wits that thinke they have thee, doe very oft prove
		fooles: and I that am sure I lacke thee, may passe for a
		wise man.
		For what saies Quinapalus, [3] Better a witty foole,
		then a foolish wit.
35		God blesse thee Lady.
	Olivia	Take the foole away.
	Clowne	Do you not heare fellowes, take away the Ladie.
	Olivia	Go too, y'are a dry foole: Ile no more of you: be-
		sides you grow dis-honest.
40	**Clowne**	Two faults Madona, that drinke & good counsell
		wil amend: for give the dry foole drink, then is the foole
		not dry: bid the dishonest man mend himself, if he mend,
		he is no longer dishonest; if hee cannot, let the Botcher
		mend him: any thing that's mended, is but patch'd: vertu
45		that transgresses, is but patcht with sinne, and sin that a-
		mends, is but patcht with vertue.
		If that this simple
		Sillogisme will serve, so: if it will not, what remedy?
		As there is no true Cuckold but calamity, so beauties a
50		flower; The Lady bad take away the foole, therefore I
		say againe, take her away.
	Olivia	Sir, I bad them take away you.

R 257 - b

[SD]1 since F1 directs Maria to make an entry later in the scene with the announcement of the disguised Viola's entry, most modern texts suggest she leaves now, though, with her concern for the Clowne, and the fact that - according to most modern texts - Olivia enters accompanied by Attendants, it is very possible that Maria stays for a while to see how the Clowne handles the situation

[SD]2 most modern texts indicate Olivia enters accompanied by Attendants

[PCT]3 most modern texts place this next phrase within quotation marks, suggesting the Clowne is quoting a saying

Clowne		Misprision in the highest degree.
55		Lady, *Cucullus non facit monachum* : that's as much to say, as I weare not motley in my braine : good Madona, give mee leave to prove you a foole.
	Olivia	Can you do it?
	Clowne	Dexteriously, good Madona.
60	**Olivia**	Make your proofe.
	Clowne	I must catechize you for it Madona, Good my Mouse of vertue answer mee.
	Olivia	Well sir, for want of other idlenesse, Ile bide your proofe.
65	**Clowne**	Good Madona, why mournst thou?
	Olivia	Good foole, for my brothers death.
	Clowne	I thinke his soule is in hell, Madona.
	Olivia	I know his soule is in heaven, foole.
70	**Clowne**	The more foole (Madona) to mourne for your Brothers soule, being in heaven.
		Take away the Foole, Gentlemen.
	Olivia	What thinke you of this foole Malvolio, doth he not mend?
75	**Malvolio**	Yes, and shall do, till the pangs of death shake him : Infirmity that decaies the wise, doth ever make the better foole.
	Clowne	God send you sir, a speedie Infirmity, for the better increasing your folly : Sir Toby will be sworn that I am no Fox, but he wil not passe his word for two pence that you are no Foole.
80		
	Olivia	How say you to that Malvolio?
	Malvolio	I marvell your Ladyship takes delight in such a barren rascall : I saw him put down the other day, with an ordinary foole, that has no more braine then a stone.
85		

| | | Looke you now, he's out of his gard already: unles you laugh and minister occasion to him, he is gag'd. |
| | | |

Looke you now, he's out of his gard already: unles you
laugh and minister occasion to him, he is gag'd.

                        I protest
I take these Wisemen, that crow so at these set kinde of

90   fooles, no better then the fooles Zanies.

Olivia   O you are sicke of selfe-love Malvolio, and taste
with a distemper'd appetite.

                      To be generous, guitlesse,[1]
and of free disposition, is to take those things for Bird-

95   bolts, that you deeme Cannon bullets: There is no slan-
der in an allow'd foole, though he do nothing but rayle;
nor no rayling, in a knowne discreet man, though hee do
nothing but reprove.

Clowne   Now Mercury indue thee with leasing, for thou

100   speak'st well of fooles.

ENTER MARIA

Maria   Madam, there is at the gate, a young Gentleman, much desires to speake with you.

Olivia   From the Count Orsino, is it?

Maria   I know not (Madam) 'tis a faire young man, and

105   well attended.

Olivia   Who of my people hold him in delay?

Maria   Sir Toby Madam, your kinsman.

Olivia   Fetch him off I pray you, he speakes nothing but
madman: Fie on him. [2]

110   Go you Malvolio; If it be a suit
from the Count, I am sicke, or not at home.

                               What you
will, to dismisse it.

[Exit Malvo{lio}]

Now you see sir, how your fooling growes old, & peo-

115   ple dislike it.

L 258 - b : 1. 5. 86 - 111

[1] F3/most modern texts = 'guitlesse', F1-2 = 'guitlesse'

[2] F1 provides an entry for Maria later in the scene, once Malvolio calls for her, line 175; thus most modern texts suggest she exits here

17

Clowne	Thou hast spoke for us (Madona) as if thy eldest sonne should be a foole: whose[†1] scull, Jove cramme with braines, for heere he comes.	

[Enter Sir Toby] [2] [3]

	One of thy kin has a most weake *Pia-mater*.	L 258 - b
120	Olivia	By mine honor halfe drunke. What is he at the gate Cosin?
	Toby	A Gentleman.
125	Olivia	A Gentleman? What Gentleman?
	Toby	'Tis a Gentleman heere. [4] A plague o'these pickle herring: How now Sot.
	Clowne	Good Sir Toby. [5]
130	Olivia	Cosin, Cosin, how have you come so earely by this Lethargie?
	Toby	Letcherie, I defie Letchery: there's one at the gate.
	Olivia	I marry, what is he?
135	Toby	Let him be the divell and he will, I care not: give me faith say I. Well, it's all one.

[Exit]

	Olivia	What's a drunken man like, foole?
140	Clowne	Like a drown'd man, a foole, and a madde man: One draught above heate, makes him a foole, the second maddes him, and a third drownes him.

L 258 - b / R 258 - b : 1. 5. 112 - 133

[W] [1] F1 = 'wh ose', F2/most modern texts = 'whose'

[UE] [2] with the entry being unusually set alongside the text instead of being centred on a separate line, perhaps Toby is trying to sneak by and not draw attention to himself, but in this he is unsuccessful; see the following footnote for a possible reason why

[SD] [3] perhaps as a justification for the following lines, most modern texts suggest Toby is staggering

[SD] [4] perhaps as a justification for the following line, most modern texts suggest Toby belches or hiccups

[PCT] [5] some modern texts replace the period of Ff with a dash, suggesting Olivia interrupts the Clowne

18

	Olivia	Go thou and seeke the Crowner, and let him sitte
		o'my Coz : for he's in the third degree of drinke : hee's
		drown'd : go looke after him.

| 145 | Clowne | He is but mad yet Madona, and the foole shall |
| | | looke to the madman. [1] |

ENTER MALVOLIO

	Malvolio	Madam, yond young fellow sweares hee will
		speake with you.
150		I told him you were sicke, he takes on
		him to understand so much, and therefore comes to speak
		with you.
		I told him you were asleepe, he seems to have
		a fore knowledge of that too, and therefore comes to
		speake with you.
155		What is to be said to him Ladie, hee's
		fortified against any deniall.

| | Olivia | Tell him, he shall not speake with me. |

	Malvolio	Ha's beene told so : and hee sayes hee'l stand at
		your doore like a Sheriffes post, and be the supporter to
160		a bench, but hee'l speake with you.

| | Olivia | What kinde o'man is he? |

| | Malvolio | Why of mankinde. |

| | Olivia | What manner of man? |

| | Malvolio | Of verie ill manner : hee'l speake with you, will |
| 165 | | you, or no. |

| | Olivia | Of what personage, and yeeres is he? |

	Malvolio	Not yet old enough for a man, nor yong enough
		for a boy : as a squash is before tis a pescod, or a Codling
		when tis almost an Apple : Tis with him in standing wa-
170		ter, betweene boy and man.
		He is verie well-favour'd,
		and he speakes verie shrewishly : One would thinke his
		mothers milke were scarse out of him.

| | Olivia | Let him approach : Call in my Gentlewoman. |

R 258 - b : 1. 5. 134 - 163

[SD]1 most modern texts add an exit for the Clowne

175	**Malvolio**	Gentlewoman, my Lady calles.

[Exit]
ENTER MARIA

Olivia	Give me my vaile: come throw it ore my face, Wee'l once more heare Orsinos Embassie.
	<center>ENTER VIOLENTA [1]</center>
Viola	The honorable Ladie of the house, which is she?
Olivia	Speake to me, I shall answer for her: your will. [2]

180	**Viola**	Most radiant, exquisite, and unmatchable beau- tie.
		I pray you tell me if this bee the Lady of the house, for I never saw her.
185		I would bee loath to cast away my speech: for besides that it is excellently well pend, I have taken great paines to con it.
		Good Beauties, let mee su- staine no scorne; I am very comptible, even to the least sinister usage.
190	**Olivia**	Whence came you sir?
	Viola	I can say little more then I have studied, & that question's out of my part.
		Good gentle one, give mee modest assurance, if you be the Ladie of the house, that may proceede in my speech.
195		[3]
	Olivia	Are you a Comedian?
	Viola	No my profound heart: and yet (by the verie phangs of malice, I sweare) I am not that I play.
200		Are you the Ladie of the house?
	Olivia	If I do not usurpe my selfe, I am.

R 258 - b

[N] [1] F2 and most modern texts = 'Viola', F1 = 'Violenta'

[VP] [2] Ff's opening could be set as verse (10/1012 or 13/11 syllables), which Viola cannot continue as she starts her praise (too nervous to keep to grace and dignity perhaps?): most modern texts set the sequence in the style of the rest of the scene to date, prose

[W] [3] F2 and most modern texts = 'I', F1 omits the word

	Viola	Most certaine, if you are she, you do usurp your selfe : for what is yours to bestowe, is, not yours to re-serve.
205		But this is from my Commission : I will on with my speech in your praise, and then shew you the heart of my message.
	Olivia	Come to what is important in't : I forgive you the praise.
210	**Viola**	Alas, I tooke great paines to studie it, and 'tis Poeticall.
	Olivia	It is the more like to be feigned, I pray you keep it in.
215		I heard you were sawcy at my gates, & allowd your approach rather to wonder at you, then to heare you.
		If you be not mad, be gone : if you have reason, be breefe : 'tis not that time of Moone with me, to make one in so skipping a dialogue.
220	**Maria**	Will you hoyst sayle sir, here lies your way.
	Viola	No good swabber, I am to hull here a little lon-ger.
		Some mollification for your Giant, sweete Ladie ; tell me your minde, I am a messenger.
225	**Olivia**	Sure you have some hiddeous matter to deliver, when the curtesie of it is so fearefull.
		Speake your office.
	Viola	It alone concernes your eare : I bring no over-ture of warre, no taxation of homage ; I hold the Olyffe in my hand : my words are as full of peace, as matter.
230		

	Olivia	Yet you began rudely.
		What are you?
		What would you? [1]

	Viola	The rudenesse that hath appear'd in mee, have I
235		learn'd from my entertainment.
		What I am, and what I would, are as secret as maiden-head : to your eares, Di-vinity ; to any others, prophanation.

L 259 - b : 1. 5. 187 - 217

LS/VP [1] set in the middle of a column where white space would not be a problem, the Ff setting offers a pause at the end of the first line as if Olivia might be waiting for replies to each of her questions: there is also the possibility that the speech might be in verse: most modern texts set the speech as continuous prose

Olivia	[1]	Give us the place alone,
240		We will heare this divinitie. [2]
		Now sir, what is your text?

Viola	Most sweet Ladie. [3]

Olivia	A comfortable doctrine, and much may bee saide
	of it.
245	Where lies your Text?

Viola	In Orsinoes bosome.

Olivia	In his bosome?
	In what chapter of his bosome?

Viola	To answer by the method, in the first of his hart.

250	Olivia	O, I have read it : it is heresie.
		Have you no more
		to say?

Viola	Good Madam, let me see your face.

Olivia	Have you any Commission from your Lord, to
255	negotiate with my face : you are now out of your Text :
	but we will draw the Curtain, and shew you the picture. [4]
	Looke you sir, such a one I was this present : Ist not well
	done?

Viola	Excellently done, if God did all.

260	Olivia	'Tis in graine sir, 'twill endure winde and wea-
		ther.

Viola	[5]	Tis beauty truly blent, whose red and white,
		Natures owne sweet, and cunning hand laid on :
		Lady, you are the cruell'st shee alive,
265		If you will leade these graces to the grave,
		And leave the world no copie.

L 259 - b : 1. 5. 218 - 243

LS/VP [1] Ff set a short (possibly verse) line, the gap suggesting Olivia waits a moment before deciding to dismiss her women so as to hear the 'Divinity' all by herself (though she does markedly reduce Viola's pronunciation of the word 'Divinity' to the more prosaic 'divinitie')

SD [2] most modern texts direct all but Olivia and Viola to leave

PCT [3] some modern texts replace the period of Ff with a dash, suggesting Olivia interrupts Viola

SD [4] most modern texts add a stage direction that Olivia unveils herself

VP [5] it is interesting to note that at the sight of her rival's face, Viola moves from verse to prose: Olivia does not follow suit until she wants the details as to 'how' Orsino 'loves' her

Olivia	O sir, I will not be so hard-hearted: I will give
	out divers scedules of my beautie.
	It shalbe [1] Inventoried
270	and every particle and utensile labell'd to my will: As,
	Item two lippes indifferent redde, Item two grey eyes,
	with lids to them: Item, one necke, one chin, & so forth.
	Were you sent hither to praise me?

L 259 - b

Viola	I see you what you are, you are too proud:
275	But if you were the divell, you are faire:
	My Lord, and master loves you: O such love
	Could be but recompenc'd, though you were crown'd

The non-pareil of beautie.

Olivia	How does he love me?
280	**Viola** With adorations, fertill teares, [2]

With groanes that thunder love, with sighes of fire.

Olivia	Your Lord does know my mind, I cannot love him [3]
	Yet I suppose him vertuous, know him noble,
	Of great estate, of fresh and stainlesse youth;
285	In voyces well divulg'd, free, learn'd, and valiant,
	And in dimension, and the shape of nature,
	A gracious person; But yet I cannot love him:
	He might have tooke his answer long ago.

Viola	If I did love you in my masters flame,
290	With such a suffring, such a deadly life:
	In your deniall, I would finde no sence,
	I would not understand it.

Olivia	Why, what would you?

Viola	Make me a willow Cabine at your gate,
295	And call upon my soule within the house,
	Write loyall Cantons of contemned love,
	And sing them lowd even in the dead of night:
	Hallow your name to the reverberate hilles,
	And make the babling Gossip of the aire,
300	Cry out Olivia: O you should not rest
	Betweene the elements of ayre, and earth,
	But you should pittie me.

---

[1] F1 = 'shalbe', F2/most modern texts = 'shall be'

[2] the actor has choice as to which two of these three short lines may be joined as one line of split verse

[3] F1 - 2 set no punctuation as if Viola's (exasperated?) explanation runs away with her: F3 gives her much more self-control by setting a comma: most modern texts set a period

	Olivia	You might do much : [1] What is your Parentage?
305	**Viola**	Above my fortunes, yet my state is well : I am a Gentleman.
	Olivia	Get you to your Lord : I cannot love him : let him send no more, Unlesse (perchance) you come to me againe,
310		To tell me how he takes it : Fare you well : I thanke you for your paines : spend this for mee.
	Viola	I am no feede poast, Lady ; keepe your purse, My Master, not my selfe, lackes recompence.
315		Love make his heart of flint, that you shal love, And let your fervour like my masters be, Plac'd in contempt : Farwell fayre crueltie.

[Exit]

	Olivia	What is your Parentage?
		Above my fortunes, yet my state is well ; I am a Gentleman.
320		Ile be sworne thou art, Thy tongue, thy face, thy limbes, actions, and spirit, Do give thee five-fold blazon : not too fast : soft, soft, Unlesse the Master were the man.
		How now?
325		Even so quickly may one catch the plague?
		Me thinkes I feele this youths perfections With an invisible, and subtle stealth To creepe in at mine eyes.
		Well, let it be.
330		What hoa, Malvolio.

ENTER MALVOLIO

	Malvolio	Heere Madam, at your service.
	Olivia	Run after that same peevish Messenger The Countes [2] man : he left this Ring behinde him Would I, or not : tell him, Ile none of it.

R 259 - b : 1. 5. 276 - 302

[1] most modern texts add this to Viola's previous short line thus creating a single split line of verse:
however, dramatically it may be more interesting to allow three short lines to follow one another with the
appropriate (shocked) pauses

[2] most modern texts = 'County's', F1 = 'Countes', F2 - 4 = 'Counts'

335   Desire him not to flatter with his Lord,
Nor hold him up with hopes, I am not for him:
If that the youth will come this way to morrow,
Ile give him reasons for't: hie thee Malvolio.

Malvolio   Madam, I will.

[Exit]

340   **Olivia**   I do I know not what, and feare to finde
Mine eye too great a flatterer for my minde: R 259 - b
Fate, shew thy force, our selves we do not owe,
What is decreed, must be: and be this so.

[Finis, Actus primus]

Actus Secundus, Scæna prima

ENTER ANTONIO & SEBASTIAN

Antonio Will you stay no longer: nor will you not that
I go with you.

Sebastian By your patience, no: my starres shine darkely
over me; the malignancie of my fate, might perhaps di-
5 stemper yours; therefore I shall crave of you your leave,
that I may beare my evils alone.
          It were a bad recom-
pence for your love, to lay any of them on you.

Antonio Let me yet know of you, whither you are bound.

10 **Sebastian** No sooth sir: my determinate voyage is meere
extravagancie.
       But I perceive in you so excellent a touch
of modestie, that you will not extort from me, what I am
willing to keepe in: therefore it charges me in manners,
15 the rather to expresse my selfe: you must know of mee
then Antonio, my name is Sebastian (which I call'd Rodo-
rigo) my father was that Sebastian of Messaline, whom I
know you have heard of.
         He left behinde him, my selfe,
20 and a sister, both borne in an houre: if the Heavens[†1] had
beene pleas'd, would we had so ended.
           But you sir, al-
ter'd that, for some houre before you tooke me from the
breach of the sea, was my sister drown'd.

25 **Antonio** Alas the day.

Sebastian A Lady sir, though it was said shee much resem-
bled me, was yet of many accounted beautiful: but thogh
I could not with such estimable wonder over-farre beleeve that, yet thus farre I will boldly publish her, shee
30 bore a mind that envy could not but call faire: Shee is
drown'd already sir with salt water, though I seeme to
drowne her remembrance againe with more.

[W] [1] F1 = 'Heanens', F2 and most modern texts = 'Heavens'

	Antonio	Pardon me sir, your bad entertainment.
	Sebastian	O good Antonio, forgive me your trouble.
35	Antonio	If you will not murther me for my love, let mee be your servant.
	Sebastian	If you will not undo what you have done, that is kill him, whom you have recover'd, desire it not.

                                                                          Fare

40   ye well at once, my bosome is full of kindnesse, and I
                            am yet so neere the manners of my mother, that upon the
                            least occasion more, mine eyes will tell tales of me : I am
                            bound to the Count Orsino's Court, farewell.

[Exit]

	Antonio	The gentlenesse of all the gods go with thee :
45		I have many enemies in Orsino's Court,
		Else would I very shortly see thee there :
		But come what may, I do adore thee so,
		That danger shall seeme sport, and I will go.

[Exit]

Scæna Secunda

ENTER VIOLA AND MALVOLIO, AT SEVERALL DOORES

	Malvolio	Were not you ev'n now, with the Countesse O- livia?
	Viola	Even now sir, on a moderate pace, I have since a- riv'd but hither.
5	**Malvolio**	She returnes this Ring to you (sir) you might have saved mee my paines, to have taken it away your selfe.

She adds moreover, that you should put your Lord   L 260 - b
into a desperate assurance, she will none of him.

10   And one
thing more, that you be never so hardie to come againe
in his affaires, unlesse it bee to report your Lords taking
of this : receive it so.

	Viola	She tooke the Ring of me, Ile none of it.
15	**Malvolio**	Come sir, you peevishly threw it to her : and her will is, it should be so return'd : If it bee worth stoo- ping for, there it lies, in your eye : if not, bee it his that findes it.

[Exit]

	Viola	I left no Ring with her : what meanes this Lady?

20   Fortune forbid my out-side have not charm'd her :
She made good view of me, indeed so much,
That [1] me thought her eyes had lost her tongue,
For she did speake in starts distractedly.

She loves me sure, the cunning of her passion
25   Invites me in this churlish messenger :
None of my Lords Ring?
                        Why he sent her none ;
I am the man, if it be so, as tis,

L 260 - b / R 260 - b   :   2. 2. 1 - 25

[w] [1] F2 and most modern texts = 'sure' (thus extending the line to 10 syllables), F1 omits the word

Poore Lady, she were better love a dreame:
30   Disguise, I see thou art a wickednesse,
Wherein the pregnant enemie does much.

How easie is it, for the proper false
In womens waxen hearts to set their formes:
Alas, O[1] frailtie is the cause, not wee,
35   For such as we are made, if[2] such we bee:
How will this fadge?
                My master loves her deerely,
And I (poore monster) fond as much on him:
And she (mistaken) seemes to dote on me:
40   What will become of this?
                    As I am man,
My state is desperate for my maisters love:
As I am woman (now alas the day)
What thriftlesse sighes shall poore Olivia breath?

45   O time, thou must untangle this, not I,
It is too hard a knot for me t'unty.[3]

R 260 - b : 2. 2. 26 - 41

[W][1] F2 and most modern texts = 'our', F1 = 'O'

[W][2] most modern texts = 'made of,', Ff = 'made, if': thus, combining this and the previous footnote, modern texts suggest the two lines should read as

        Alas, our frailtie is the cause, not we,
        For such as we are made of, such we be.

[SD][3] most modern texts add an exit for Viola

Scœna Tertia

ENTER SIR TOBY, AND SIR ANDREW

Toby   Approach Sir Andrew : not to bee a bedde after
midnight, is to be up betimes, and *Deliculo surgere*, thou
know'st. [1]

Andrew   Nay by my troth I know not : but I know, to
5   be up late, is to be up late.

Toby   A false conclusion : I hate it as an unfill'd Canne.

To be up after midnight, and to go to bed then is early :
so that to go to bed after midnight, is to goe to bed betimes.
10   Does not our lives consist of the foure Elements?

Andrew   Faith so they say, but I thinke it rather consists
of eating and drinking.

Toby   Th'art a scholler ; let us therefore eate and drinke. [2]
15   Marian I say, a stoope of wine.

ENTER CLOWNE

Andrew   Heere comes the foole yfaith.

Clowne   How now my harts : Did you never see the Pic-
ture of we three?

Toby   Welcome asse, now let's have a catch.

20 **Andrew**   By my troth the foole has an excellent breast.
                                        I
had rather then forty shillings I had such a legge, and so
sweet a breath to sing, as the foole has.

[1] some modern texts replace the period of Ff with a dash, suggesting Andrew interrupts Toby
[2] F1 sets what seems to be a blurred period, which most modern texts follow: F2 sets a comma

		Insooth thou wast
25		in very gracious fooling last night, when thou spok'st of
		Pigrogromitus, of the Vapians passing the Equinoctial of
		Queubus: 'twas very good yfaith: I sent thee sixe pence	R 260-b
		for thy Lemon,[1] hadst it?

Clowne   I did impeticos thy gratillity: for Malvolios nose
is no Whip-stocke.
                         My Lady has a white hand, and the
Mermidons are no bottle-ale houses.

Andrew   Excellent: Why this is the best fooling, when
all is done.
Now a song.

Toby   Come on, there is sixe pence for you.
                                   Let's have
a song.

Andrew   There's a testrill of me too: if one knight give a[2]

Clowne   Would you have a love-song, or a song of good
life?

Toby   A love song, a love song.

Andrew   I, I.
                I care not for good life.

[Clowne sings][3]

O Mistris mine where are you roming?

O stay and heare, your true loves coming,
That can sing both high and low.

Trip no further prettie sweeting.

Journeys end in lovers meeting,
Every wise mans sonne doth know.

Andrew   Excellent good, ifaith.

Toby   Good, good.

R 260 - b / L 261 - b : 2. 3. 22 - 46

[W][1] most modern texts = 'leman' (viz. 'sweetheart'), F1 = 'Lemon'

[PCT][2] some modern texts follow F2 and set a dash, suggesting the Clowne interrupts Andrew: F1 omits any final
punctuation

[M/SPD][3] the last four lines of the first verse and all the second verse of the song are set in the reversed heartbeat
pattern of ritual and magic predominantly found in *The Tragedie of Macbeth* and *A Midsommer Nights
Dreame*: this might suggest the song gains extra power once Feste reaches the idea of 'true love'

	Clowne	*What is love, tis not heereafter,*
		Present mirth, hath present laughter :
55		*What's to come, is still unsure.*
		In delay there lies no plentie,
		Then come kisse me sweet and twentie :
		Youths a stuffe will not endure.

	Andrew	A mellifluous voyce, as I am true knight.
60	Toby	A contagious breath.
	Andrew	Very sweet, and contagious ifaith.
	Toby	To heare by the nose, it is dulcet in contagion. But shall we make the Welkin dance indeed?

Shall wee

65 rowze the night-Owle in a Catch, that will drawe three soules out of one Weaver?

Shall we do that?

	Andrew	And you love me, let's doo't : I am dogge at a Catch.
70	Clowne	Byrlady sir, and some dogs will catch well.
	Andrew	Most certaine : Let our Catch be, *Thou Knave*.
	Clowne	*Hold thy peace, thou Knave* knight. [1]

I shall be con-

strain'd in't, to call thee knave, Knight.

75	Andrew	'Tis not the first time I have constrained one to call me knave.

Begin foole : it begins, *Hold thy peace*.

	Clowne	I shall never begin if I hold my peace.
	Andrew	Good ifaith : Come begin.

[Catch sung]
ENTER MARIA

80	Maria	What a catterwalling doe you keepe heere?

If

my Ladie have not call'd up her Steward Malvolio, and bid him turne you out of doores, never trust me.

L 261 - b : 2. 3. 47 - 74

[PCT][1] most modern texts replace Ff's period with a question mark: Ff's setting allows Feste's set up for the punch line a little more subtlety

Toby	My Lady's a Catayan, we are politicians, Malvolios	
85	a Peg-a-ramsie, and *Three merry men be wee.* [1]	
	Am not I	
	consanguinious?	
	Am I not of her blood : tilly vally.	
	La-	
90	die, *There dwelt a man in Babylon, Lady, Lady.*	

Clowne	Beshrew me, the knights in admirable fooling.	

Andrew	I, he do's well enough if he be dispos'd, and so	
	do I too : he does it with a better grace, but I do it more	
	naturall.	

95	**Toby**	*O the twelfe day of December.*

Maria	For the love o'God peace.	

ENTER MALVOLIO

Malvolio	My Masters are you mad?	
	Or what are you?	
	Have you no wit, manners, nor honestie, but to gabble	
100	like Tinkers at this time of night?	
	Do yee make an Ale-	
	house of my Ladies house, that ye squeak out your Cozi-	
	ers Catches without any mitigation or remorse of voice?	
	Is there no respect of place, persons, nor time in you?	L 261-b

105	**Toby**	We did keepe time sir in our Catches.
		Snecke up.

Malvolio	Sir Toby, I must be round with you.	
	My Lady	
	bad me tell you, that though she harbors you as her kins-	
110	man, she's nothing ally'd to your disorders.	
	If you can	
	separate your selfe and your misdemeanors, you are wel-	
	come to the house : if not, and it would please you to take	
	leave of her, she is very willing to bid you farewell.	

115	**Toby**	• [2] Farewell deere heart, since I must needs be gone.

LS/SPD [1]   L 261-b/R 261-b : 2. 3. 75 - 103

for the rest of the scene, most modern texts suggest that when F1 sets italics, the character is singing

SPD [2] research has shown that within the next eleven lines the 'dialogue' for Toby and the Clowne is taken
from a contemporary song (see *The New Cambridge Shakespeare Twelfth Night*, page 77, footnote to lines 86-
96, and *The Riverside Shakespeare*, page 441, ops. cit.): thus, the following sequences with the symbol •
indicate where modern texts suggest the lines should be sung: however, the F1 text suggests that while the
song may be quoted from this point on, the actual singing does not occur until the commencement of the
italics

Maria		Nay good Sir Toby.
Clowne	•	His eyes do shew his dayes are almost done.
Malvolio		Is't even so?
Toby	•	But I will never dye.
120 **Clowne**	•	Sir Toby there you lye.
Malvolio		This is much credit to you.
Toby		*Shall I bid him go.*
Clowne		*What and if you do?*
Toby		*Shall I bid him go, and spare not?*
125 **Clowne**		*O no, no, no, no, you dare not.*

Toby   Out o'tune [1] sir, ye lye: Art any more then a Steward?
Dost thou thinke because thou art vertuous, there
shall be no more Cakes and Ale?

130 **Clowne**   Yes by S. Anne, and Ginger shall bee hotte y'th
mouth too. [2]

Toby   Th'art i'th right.
Goe sir, rub your Chaine with
crums.
135   A stope of Wine Maria.

Malvolio   Mistris Mary, if you priz'd my Ladies favour
at any thing more then contempt, you would not give
meanes for this uncivill rule ; she shall know of it by this
hand.

[Exit]

140 **Maria**   Go shake your eares.

Andrew   'Twere as good a deede as to drink when a mans
a hungrie, to challenge him the field, and then to breake
promise with him, and make a foole of him.

---

[w][1] though some modern texts agree with Ff and print this as 'tune', one interesting gloss picks up an earlier
comment from Toby to Malvolio (line 105) and sets 'time'

[SD][2] the Clowne has no more lines in the scene, and thus some modern texts take it upon themselves to direct
him to leave after this line, which, dramatically, seems a very weak and unmotivated choice, unless he is
running away to avoid further conflict

145	**Toby**	Doo't knight, Ile write thee a Challenge : or Ile, deliver thy indignation to him by word of mouth.
	Maria	Sweet Sir Toby be patient for to night : Since the youth of the Counts was to day with my Lady, she is much out of quiet.
150		For Monsieur Malvolio, let me alone with him : If I do not gull him into an ayword,[1] and make him a common recreation, do not thinke I have witte e- nough to lye straight in my bed : I know I can do it.
	Toby	Possesse us, possesse us, tell us something of him.
	Maria	Marrie sir, sometimes he is a kinde of Puritane.
155	**Andrew**	O, if I thought that, Ide beate him like a dogge.
	Toby	What for being a Puritan, thy exquisite reason, deere knight.
	Andrew	I have no exquisite reason for't, but I have reason good enough.
160	**Maria**	The div'll a Puritane that hee is, or any thing constantly but a time-pleaser, an affection'd Asse, that cons State without booke, and utters it by great swarths.
165		The best perswaded of himselfe : so cram'd (as he thinkes) with excellencies, that it is his grounds of faith, that all that looke on him, love him : and on that vice in him, will my revenge finde notable cause to worke.
	Toby	What wilt thou do?
170	**Maria**	I will drop in his way some obscure Epistles of love, wherein by the colour of his beard, the shape of his legge, the manner of his gate, the expressure of his eye, forehead, and complection, he shall finde himselfe most feelingly personated.
175		I can write very like my Ladie your Neece, on a forgotten matter wee can hardly make distinction of our hands.
	Toby	Excellent, I smell a device.
	Andrew	I hav't in my nose too.

---

[1] some modern texts set 'a nayward', others follow Ff and set 'an ayward'

	Toby	He shall thinke by the Letters that thou wilt drop	R 261 - b
180		that they come from my Neece, and that shee's in love with him.	
	Maria	My purpose is indeed a horse of that colour.	
	Andrew	And your horse now would make him an Asse.	
	Maria	Asse, I doubt not.	
	Andrew	O twill be admirable.	
185	Maria	Sport royall I warrant you: I know my Phy-sicke will worke with him, I will plant you two, and let the Foole make a third, where he shall finde the Letter: observe his construction of it: For this night to bed, and dreame on the event: Farewell.	

[Exit]

190	Toby	Good night Penthisilea.
	Andrew	Before me she's a good wench.
	Toby	She's a beagle true bred, and one that adores me: what o'that?
	Andrew	I was ador'd once too.
195	Toby	Let's to bed knight: Thou hadst neede send for more money.
	Andrew	If I cannot recover your Neece, I am a foule way out.
	Toby	Send for money knight, if thou hast her not i'th
200		end, call me Cut.
	Andrew	If I do not, never trust me, take it how you will.
	Toby	Come, come, Ile go burne some Sacke, tis too late to go to bed now: Come knight, come knight.

[Exeunt]

Scena Quarta

Duke	Give me some Musick; [2] Now good morow frends.

Now good Cesario, but that peece of song,
That old and Anticke song we heard last night;
Me thought it did releeve my passion much,
5   More then light ayres, and recollected termes
Of these most briske[†3] and giddy-paced times.

Come, but one verse.

Curio   He is not heere (so please your Lordshippe) that
        should sing it?

10 **Duke**   Who was it?

Curio   Feste the Jester my Lord, a foole that the Ladie
        Oliviaes Father tooke much delight in.
                            He is about the
        house.

15 **Duke**   Seeke him out, [4] and play the tune the while.

MUSICKE PLAYES

Come hither Boy, if ever thou shalt love
In the sweet pangs of it, remember me:
For such as I am, all true Lovers are,
Unstaid and skittish in all motions else,
20   Save in the constant image of the creature
That is belov'd.
                  How dost thou like this tune?

[SD1] most modern texts expand 'others' to include a combination of Lords, Attendants, and Musicians

[SD2] various stage directions have been added here: among the most prevalent are that the Musicians either rush in from offstage, or that they are already on-stage and just step forward

[W3] F1 = 'b riske', F2/most modern texts = 'briske'

[SD4] most modern texts add a stage direction here that someone (usually Curio) exits to find the Clowne

	Viola	It gives a verie eccho to the seate Where love is thron'd.
25	**Duke**	Thou dost speake masterly, My life upon't, yong though thou art, thine eye Hath staid upon some favour that it loves : Hath it not boy?
	Viola	A little, by your favour.
30	**Duke**	What kinde of woman ist?
	Viola	Of your complection.
	Duke	She is not worth thee then. 　　　　　　　　　What yeares ifaith?
	Viola	About your yeeres my Lord.
35	**Duke**	Too old by heaven : Let still the woman take L 262 - b An elder then her selfe, so weares she to him ; So swayes she levell in her husbands heart : For boy, however we do praise our selves, Our fancies are more giddie and unfirme,
40		More longing, wavering, sooner lost and worne,[1] Then womens are.
	Viola	I thinke it well my Lord.
	Duke	Then let thy Love be yonger then thy selfe, Or thy affection cannot hold the bent :
45		For women are as Roses, whose faire flowre Being once displaid, doth fall that verie howre.
	Viola	And so they are : alas, that they are so : To die, even when they to perfection grow.

ENTER CURIO & CLOWNE

	Duke	O fellow come, the song we had last night :
50		Marke it Cesario, it is old and plaine ; The Spinsters and the Knitters in the Sun, And the free maides that weave their thred with bones, Do use to chaunt it : it is silly sooth, And dallies with the innocence of love,
55		Like the old age.

---

[1] though most modern texts agree with Ff and print this as 'worne', one gloss = 'won'

	Clowne	Are you ready Sir?
	Duke	I prethee sing.

[Musicke]

THE SONG

Come away, come away death,
And in sad cypresse let me be laide.
60   *Fye* [1] *away, fie away breath,*
I am slaine by a faire cruell maide :
My shrowd of white, stuck all with Ew, [2] *° O prepare it . °*
My part of death no one so true ° did share it . °

Not a flower, not a flower sweete
65   *On my blacke coffin, let there be strewne :*
Not a friend, not a friend greet
My poore corpes, where my bones shall be throwne :
A thousand thousand sighes to save, ° lay me ô where °
Sad true lover never find my grave, ° to weepe there . ° [3]

70 **Duke**   There's for thy paines. [4]

       Clowne   No paines sir, I take pleasure in singing sir.

       Duke   Ile pay thy pleasure then.

       Clowne   Truely sir, and pleasure will be paide one time, or
                        another.

75 **Duke**   Give me now leave, to leave thee.

       Clowne   Now the melancholly God protect thee, and the
                        Tailor make thy doublet of changeable Taffata, for thy
                        minde is a very Opall.
                                        I would have men of such constan-
80   cie put to Sea, that their businesse might be every thing,
                        and their intent everie where, for that's it, that alwayes
                        makes a good voyage of nothing.
                                              Farewell.

[Exit]

SPD/W [1] some modern texts = 'Fly . . . fly', others follow Ff and set 'Fye . . . fie'

W [2] most modern texts = 'yew', F1 = 'Ew'

SPD [3] some modern texts split the song lines even more by the inner rhyme scheme, as the symbols ° show

SD [4] most modern texts add a stage direction that the Duke gives money to the Clowne

	Duke	Let all the rest give place: [1] Once more Cesario,
85		Get thee to yond same soveraigne crueltie:
		Tell her my love, more noble then the world
		Prizes not quantitie of dirtie lands,
		The parts that fortune hath bestow'd upon her: [2]
		Tell her I hold as giddily as Fortune:
90		But 'tis that miracle, and Queene of Jems
		That nature prankes her in, attracts my soule.

| | Viola | But if she cannot love you sir. |

| | Duke | It [3] cannot be so answer'd. |

	Viola	Sooth but you must.
95		Say that some Lady, as perhappes there is,
		Hath for your love as great a pang of heart
		As you have for Olivia: you cannot love her:
		You tel her so: Must she not then be answer'd?

	Duke	There is no womans sides R 262 - b
100		Can bide the beating of so strong a passion,
		As love doth give my heart: no womans heart
		So bigge, to hold so much, they lacke retention.
		Alas, their love may be call'd appetite,
		No motion of the Liver, but the Pallat,
105		That suffer [4] surfet, cloyment, and revolt,
		But mine is all as hungry as the Sea,
		And can digest as much, make no compare
		Betweene that love a woman can beare me,
		And that I owe Olivia.

| 110 | Viola | I but I know. [5] |

| | Duke | What dost thou knowe? |

| | Viola | Too well what love women to men may owe: |
| | | In faith they are as true of heart, as we. |

R 262 - b / L 263 - b : 2. 4. 78 - 106

[SD]1 as in Act One Scene 4, most modern texts suggest all withdraw from the Duke and Viola

[PCT]2 F1 sets a colon as Orsino is working hard to find the proper description: F2 softens his search by setting a comma, while some modern texts omit the punctuation completely

[W]3 most modern texts = 'I', Ff = 'It'

[W]4 most modern texts = 'suffers', Ff = 'suffer'

[PCT]5 some modern texts replace the period of Ff with a dash, suggesting the Duke interrupts Viola: however, her previous eight syllable line suggests a pause somewhere - perhaps she cuts herself off to avoid giving herself away

My Father had a daughter lov'd a man
115   As it might be perhaps, were I a woman
I should your Lordship.

Duke   And what's her history?

Viola   A blanke my Lord : she never told her love,
But let concealment like a worme i'th budde
120   Feede on her damaske cheeke : she pin'd in thought,
And with a greene and yellow melancholly,
She sate like Patience on a Monument,
Smiling at greefe.
                        Was not this love indeede?
125   We men may say more, sweare more, but indeed
Our shewes are more then will : for still we prove
Much in our vowes, but little in our love.

Duke   But di'de thy sister of her love my Boy?

Viola   I am all the daughters of my Fathers house,
130   And all the brothers too : and yet I know not.

Sir, shall I to this Lady?

Duke   I that's the Theame,
To her in haste : give her this Jewell : say,
My love can give no place, bide no denay.

[exeunt]

Scena Quinta

ENTER SIR TOBY, SIR ANDREW, AND FABIAN

Toby	Come thy wayes Signior Fabian.
Fabian	Nay Ile come : if I loose a scruple of this sport, let me be boyl'd to death with Melancholly.
Toby	Wouldst thou not be glad to have the niggard- ly Rascally sheepe-biter, come by some notable shame?
Fabian	I would exult man : you know he brought me out o'favour with my Lady, about a Beare-baiting heere.
Toby	To anger him wee'l have the Beare againe, and we will foole him blacke and blew, shall we not sir An- drew?
Andrew	And we do not, it is pittie of our lives.

ENTER MARIA [1]

Toby	Heere comes the little villaine : How now my Mettle of India?
Maria	Get ye all three into the box tree : Malvolio's comming downe this walke, he has beene yonder i'the Sunne practising behaviour to his own shadow this halfe houre : observe him for the love of Mockerie : for I know this Letter wil make a contemplative Ideot of him. <div align="right">Close</div>in the name of jeasting,[2] lye thou there : for heere comes the Trowt, that must be caught with tickling.

[Exit]
ENTER MALVOLIO

[1] most modern texts set the entrance half a line later

[2] most modern texts add two stage directions, one for the men to hide, the other for Maria to drop a letter

	Malvolio	'Tis but Fortune, all is fortune.
		Maria once
		told me she did affect me, and I have heard her self come
25		thus neere, that should shee fancie, it should bee one of
		my complection.
		Besides she uses me with a more ex- L 263 - b
		alted respect, then any one else that followes her.
		What
30		should I thinke on't?
	Toby	Heere's an over-weening rogue.
	Fabian	Oh peace: Contemplation makes a rare Turkey
		Cocke of him, how he jets under his advanc'd plumes.
	Andrew	Slight I could so beate the Rogue.
35	Toby * [1]	Peace I say.
	Malvolio	To be Count Malvolio.
	Toby	Ah Rogue.
	Andrew	Pistoll him, pistoll him.
	Toby *	Peace, peace.
40	Malvolio	There is example for't: The Lady of the Stra-
		chy, married the yeoman of the wardrobe. * [2]
	Andrew	Fie on him Jezabel.
	Fabian	O peace, now he's deeply in: looke how imagi-
		nation blowes him.
45	Malvolio	Having beene three moneths married to her,
		sitting in my state. *
	Toby	O for a stone-bow to hit him in the eye.

L 263 - b / R 263 - b : 2. 5. 23 - 46

LS/P [1] though Ff assign both speeches thus asterisked to Toby, most modern texts reassign them to Fabian, arguing that logically the lines should belong to the latter since he appears to be the peace-keeper: while logical, there may be merit in keeping the speeches as originally assigned, thus allowing Toby to start out relatively calmly, but then begin to get (rightfully) angry as Malvolio fantasizes about leaving Olivia 'sleeping' (lines 49-50), presumably after having made love

PCT [2] some modern texts replace the period of Ff with a dash, suggesting Malvolio's speeches drift away, as he loses himself in his daydreams, allowing the watcher to speak his line unobserved: all similar modern text resetting in this scene will be marked with the symbol * without an accompanying footnote

	Malvolio	Calling my Officers about me, in my branch'd
		Velvet gowne : having come from a day bedde, where I
50		have left Olivia sleeping. *
	Toby	Fire and Brimstone.
	Fabian	O peace, peace.
	Malvolio	And then to have the humor of state : and after
		a demure travaile of regard : telling them I knowe my
55		place, as I would they should doe theirs : to aske for my
		kinsman Toby. *
	Toby	Boltes and shackles.
	Fabian	Oh peace, peace, peace, now, now.
	Malvolio	Seaven of my people with an obedient start,
60		make out for him : I frowne the while, and perchance
		winde up my watch, or play with my [1] some rich Jewell :
		Toby approaches ; curtsies there to me. *
	Toby	Shall this fellow live?
	Fabian	Though our silence be drawne from us with cars, [2]
65		yet peace.
	Malvolio	I extend my hand to him thus : quenching my
		familiar smile with an austere regard of controll. *
	Toby	And do's not Toby take you a blow o'the lippes,
		then?
70	**Malvolio**	Saying, Cosine Toby, my Fortunes having cast
		me on your Neece, give me this prerogative of speech. *
	Toby	What, what?
	Malvolio	You must amend your drunkennesse.
	Toby	Out scab.
75	**Fabian**	Nay patience, or we breake the sinewes of our
		plot?

PCT [1] most modern texts add a dash here, to allow Malvolio a silent moment to realise what he was about to play with (and most productions suggest it to be his Chain of Office, a sign of his currently subservient status) is no longer appropriate, and to hesitate before switching his day-dream to 'some rich Jewell', a much more definitive sign of his longed for wealth and power

W [2] F2 = 'with cares', F1 = 'with cars', most modern texts set the gloss, 'by th'ears'

Malvolio		Besides you waste the treasure of your time, with a foolish knight. *
Andrew		That's mee I warrant you.
80 **Malvolio**		One sir Andrew. *
Andrew		I knew 'twas I, for many do call mee foole.
Malvolio	1	What employment have we heere?
Fabian *		Now is the Woodcocke neere the gin.
Toby *	2	Oh peace, and the spirit of humors intimate reading aloud to him.

85

Malvolio		By my life this is my Ladies hand: these bee her very *C's*, her *U's*, and her *T's*, and thus makes shee her†3 great *P's*.

> It is in contempt of question her hand.

90 **Andrew**		Her *C's*, her *U's*, and her *T's*: why that?
Malvolio	4	*To the unknowne belov'd, this, and my good Wishes:* Her very Phrases: By your leave wax.

> Soft, and the impressure her Lucrece, with which she uses to seale: tis my

95 Lady: To whom should this be? 5

Fabian		This winnes him, Liver and all.	R 263 - b
Malvolio		*Jove knowes I love,° but who,° Lips do not moove,° no man must know ° 6.*

> No man must know.

100
> What followes?

The numbers alter'd: †7 No man must know,
If this should be thee Malvolio?

R 263 - b / L 264 - b : 2. 5. 77 - 102

SD 1 most modern texts add a stage direction for Malvolio to notice and/or pick up the letter

P 2 again, arguing Fabian is still the peace-keeper, some modern texts assign this speech to Fabian and the previous one to Toby (see fn. #1, page 43)

W 3 F1 = 'het', F2/most modern texts = 'her'

SD 4 most modern texts indicate Malvolio reads the outside of the letter (this script will follow Ff and set the 'letter text' in italics, thus avoiding the need to keep repeating the instruction 'read')

SD 5 most modern texts add a stage direction that here Malvolio opens the letter, though by the earlier phrase 'By your leave wax' (line 92) it might seem he has been trying to pry it open for some time

VP 6 Ff set the text as prose: some modern texts, taking Malvolio's later phrase 'here follows prose' (145-6) as their cue, set this and the next reading from the letter in verse, as the symbols ° indicate

W 7 F1 = 'alter d', F2/most modern texts = 'alter'd'

	Toby	Marrie hang thee brocke.
105	**Malvolio**	*I may command where I adore,°* but silence like a Lu-*cresse knife :* ° *With bloodlesse stroke my heart doth gore,°* M.O.A.I. doth *sway my life* . °
	Fabian	A fustian riddle.
	Toby	Excellent Wench, say I.
110	**Malvolio**	*M.O.A.I. doth sway my life.* 　　　　　　　　　Nay but first let me see, let me see, let me see.
	Fabian	What dish a [1] poyson has she drest him?
	Toby	And with what wing the stallion [2] checkes at it?
115	**Malvolio**	*I may command, where I adore* : Why shee may command me : I serve her, she is my Ladie. 　　　　　　　　　　　Why this is evident to any formall capacitie. 　　　　　　　　　　　　There is no obstruction
120		in this, and the end : What should that Alphabeticall po-sition portend, if I could make that resemble something in me? 　　　　Softly, *M.O.A.I.* *
	Toby	O I, make up that, he is now at a cold sent.
125	**Fabian**	Sowter will cry upon't for all this, though it bee as ranke as a Fox.
	Malvolio	*M.* 　　　*Malvolio, M.* why that begins my name.
130	**Fabian**	Did not I say he would worke it out, the Curre is excellent at faults.
	Malvolio	*M.* 　　　But then there is no consonancy in the sequell [3] that suffers under probation : *A.* should follow, but *O.* does.

L 264 - b : 2. 5. 103 - 131

[W][1] most modern texts = 'o', Ff = 'a'

[W][2] enlarging upon the image 'with what wing' most modern texts alter F1's 'stallion' to 'staniel' (a kestrel - a bird useless in hawking, and thus a contemptuous term when applied to a human being))

[PCT][3] for clarity most modern texts set a period to separate the two ideas: however, Malvolio is not necessarily at his most logical at the moment

135	**Fabian**	And *O* shall end, I hope.
	Toby	I, or Ile cudgell him, and make him cry *O*.
	Malvolio	And then *I.* comes behind.
	Fabian	I, and you had any eye behinde you, you might
140		see more detraction at your heeles, then Fortunes before you.
	Malvolio	*M, O, A, I.*

This simulation is not as the former:
and yet to crush this a little, it would bow to mee, for e-
very one of these Letters are in my name.

Soft, here fol-
lowes prose: *If this fall into thy hand, revolve.*

[1] In my stars
I am above thee, but be not affraid of greatnesse: Some
are become [2] great, some atcheeves [3] greatnesse, and some
have greatnesse thrust uppon em.

Thy fates open theyr
hands, let thy blood and spirit embrace them, and to in-
ure thy selfe to what thou art like to be: cast thy humble
slough, and appeare fresh.

Be opposite with a kinsman,
surly with servants: Let thy tongue tang arguments of
state; put thy selfe into the tricke of singularitie.

Shee
thus advises thee, that sighes for thee.

Remember who
commended thy yellow stockings, and wish'd to see thee [+4]
ever crosse garter'd: I say remember, goe too, thou art
made if thou desir'st to be so: If not, let me see thee a steward still, the fellow of servants, and not woorthie to
touch Fortunes fingers [5] Farewell, Shee that would alter

COMP [1] the following is the main text of the letter, and is the only section Ff do not set in italics (unlike the verse preambles and the ending postscript): this could reflect the practice of the folding 'one on top of another' of the various teasing introductory parts of the Elizabethan love letter - i.e. that the opening (italicised) parts have been folded intricately one on top of another, as will be the postscript, but once the main body of the text is reached it is completely revealed as one unit

W [2] presumably because of later text references from Malvolio (3.4.46; page 64) and Feste (5.1.403; page 99), most modern texts alter Ff's 'become' to 'borne'

W [3] F1 = 'atcheeves', F2 and most modern texts = 'atcheeve'

W [4] F1 = 'thce', F2/most modern texts = 'thee'

PCT [5] Ff set no punctuation as if Malvolio's excitement runs away with him: most modern texts set a period

services with thee, that [+1] fortunate unhappy [2] daylight and
champian discovers not more : This is open, I will bee
proud, I will reade politicke [+3] Authours, I will baffle Sir
Toby, I will wash off grosse acquaintance, I will be point
170   devise, the very man.
                              I do not now foole my selfe, to let
imagination jade mee ; for every reason excites to this,
that my Lady loves me.
                              She did commend my yellow
175   stockings of late, shee did praise my legge being crosse-
garter'd, and in this she manifests her selfe to my love, &
with a kinde of injunction drives mee to these habites of
her liking.
                     I thanke my starres, I am happy: I will bee
180   strange, stout, in yellow stockings, and crosse Garter'd,   L 264 - b
even with the swiftnesse of putting on.
                                        Jove, and my
starres be praised.
                        Heere is yet a postscript.
185   *Thou canst*
not choose but know who I am .
                              If thou entertainst my love, let
it appeare in thy smiling, thy smiles become thee well .
                                      There-
190   *fore in my presence still smile, deero [4] my sweete, I prethee .*
                                            Jove
I thanke thee, I will smile, I wil do every thing that thou
wilt have me.

[Exit]

Fabian	I will not give my part of this sport for a pensi-
195	on of thousands to be paid from the Sophy.
Toby	I could marry this wench for this device.
Andrew	So could I too.
Toby	And aske no other dowry with her, but such ano- ther jest.

[W][1] F1 = 'tht', F2 and most modern texts = 'the'

[PCT][2] here all modern texts indicate the letter is finished, usually by adding some form of punctuation, and that
Malvolio is speaking/gabbling his own thoughts

[W][3] F1 = 'pollticke', F2/most modern texts = 'politicke'

[W][4] F1 = 'deero', F2 = 'deer', most modern texts = 'dear'

ENTER MARIA [1]

200	**Andrew**	Nor I neither.
	Fabian	Heere comes my noble gull catcher.
	Toby	Wilt thou set thy foote o'my necke.
	Andrew	Or o'mine either?
205	**Toby**	Shall I play my freedome at tray-trip, and becom thy bondslave?
	Andrew	Ifaith, or I either?
	Toby	Why, thou hast put him in such a dreame, that when the image of it leaves him, he must run mad.
	Maria	Nay but say true, do's it worke upon him?
210	**Toby**	Like Aqua vite with a Midwife.
215	**Maria**	If you will then see the fruites of the sport, mark his first approach before my Lady: hee will come to her in yellow stockings, and 'tis a colour she abhorres, and crosse garter'd, a fashion shee detests: and hee will smile upon her, which will now be so unsuteable to her disposition, being addicted to a melancholly, as shee is, that it cannot but turn him into a notable contempt: if you wil see it follow me.
220	**Toby**	To the gates of Tartar, thou most excellent divell of wit.
	Andrew	Ile make one too.

[Exeunt]
[Finis Actus secundus]

R 264 - b : 2. 5. 186 - 207

[SD]1 most modern texts delay the entry for two lines

Actus Tertius, Scæna prima

ENTER VIOLA AND CLOWNE [1]

	Viola	Save thee Friend and thy Musick : dost thou live by thy Tabor?
	Clowne	No sir, I live by the Church.
	Viola	Art thou a Churchman?
5	**Clowne**	No such matter sir, I do live by the Church : For, I do live at my house, and my house dooth stand by the Church [2]
	Viola	So thou maist say the Kings [3] lyes by a begger, if a begger dwell neer him : or the Church[†][4] stands by thy Tabor, if thy Tabor stand by the Church.
10		
	Clowne	You have said sir : To see this age : A sentence is but a chev'rill glove to a good witte, how quickely the wrong side may be turn'd outward.
15	**Viola**	Nay that's certaine : they that dally nicely with words, may quickely make them wanton.
	Clowne	I would therefore my sister had had no name Sir.
	Viola	Why man?
	Clowne	Why sir, her names a word, and to dallie with that word, might make my sister wanton : But indeede, words are very Rascals, since bonds disgrac'd them.
20		
	Viola	Thy reason man?

R 264 - b

R 264 - b / L 273ᵉ - b : 3. 1. 1 - 22

[SD][1] most modern texts add to the stage direction that the Clowne is playing on both pipe and tabor

[PCT][2] F1 shows no punctuation at the end of the line, perhaps suggesting Viola interrupts him: F2 and modern texts add a period

[W][3] F2 and most modern texts = 'King', F1 = 'Kings'

[4] F1 = 'Chuech', F2/most modern texts = 'Church'

Clowne		Troth sir, I can yeeld you none without wordes, and wordes are growne so false, I am loath to prove reason with them.
25	**Viola**	I warrant thou art a merry fellow, and car'st for nothing.
	Clowne	Not so sir, I do care for something: but in my conscience sir, I do not care for you: if that be to care for nothing sir, I would it would make you invisible.
30	**Viola**	Art not thou the Lady Olivia's foole?
	Clowne	No indeed sir, the Lady Olivia has no folly, shee will keepe no foole sir, till she be married, and fooles are as like husbands, as Pilchers [1] are to Herrings, the Husbands the bigger, I am indeede not her foole, but hir corrupter of words.
35		
	Viola	I saw thee late at the Count Orsino's.
	Clowne	Foolery sir, does walke about the Orbe like the Sun, it shines every where.
		I would be sorry sir, but the
40		Foole should be as oft with your Master, as with my Mistris: I thinke I saw your wisedome there.
	Viola	Nay, and thou passe upon me, Ile no more with thee.
		Hold there's expences for thee. [2]
45	**Clowne**	Now Jove in his next commodity of hayre, send thee a beard.
	Viola	By my troth Ile tell thee, I am almost sicke for one, [3] though I would not have it grow on my chinne.
		Is
50		thy Lady within?
	Clowne	Would not a paire of these have bred sir?
	Viola	Yes being kept together, and put to use.
	Clowne	I would play Lord Pandarus of Phrygia sir, to bring a Cressida to this Troylus.

W [1] most modern texts = 'pilchards', F1 = 'Pilchers'

SD [2] most modern texts add a stage direction that Viola gives the Clowne a (single) coin

A [3] most modern texts indicate the remainder of the sentence is spoken as an aside

55	**Viola**	I understand you sir, tis well begg'd. [1]

Clowne   The matter I hope is not great sir; begging, but a
begger : Cressida was a begger.

                  My Lady is within sir.

                                              I

60   will conster to them whence you come, who you are, and
what you would are out of my welkin, I might say Element, but the word is over-worne.

                        [exit]

Viola   This fellow is wise enough to play the foole,
And to do that well, craves a kinde of wit :

65   He must obeserve their mood on whom he jests,
The quality of persons, and the time :
And [2] like the Haggard, checke at every Feather
That comes before his eye.

                      This is[†3] a practice,

70   As full of labour as a Wise-mans Art :
For folly that he wisely shewes, is fit ;
But wisemens folly falne,[4] quite taint their wit.

              ENTER SIR TOBY AND ANDREW

Toby   Save you Gentleman.

Viola   And you sir.

75   **Andrew**   *Dieu vou guard Monsieur.*[5]

Viola   *Et vouz ousie vostre serviture.*

Andrew   I hope sir, you are, and I am yours.

Toby   Will you incounter the house, my Neece is desi-
rous you should enter, if your trade be to her.

80   **Viola**   I am bound to your Neece sir, I meane she is the
list of my voyage.

[SD1] most modern texts suggest Viola gives him another coin

[▼2] though some modern texts agree with Ff and print this as 'And', one gloss = 'Not'

[▼3] F1 = 'thisis', F2/most modern texts = 'This is'

[▼4] some modern texts = 'wise men, folly falne,', F2 = 'Wise mens folly falne,', F1 = 'wisemens folly falne,'

[▼5] this is where the difference between a proofed and unproofed Folio is fascinating: the 1950's *Yale*
version shows the F1 setting as 'Monsiuer', the 1960's *Norton* shows for the same line the setting 'Móusieur'

	Toby	Taste your legges sir, put them to motion.	
	Viola	My legges do better understand me sir, then I understand what you meane by bidding me taste my legs.	
85	Toby	I meane to go sir, to enter.	
	Viola	I will answer you with gate and entrance, but we are prevented.	

ENTER OLIVIA, AND GENTLEWOMAN

		Most excellent accomplish'd Lady, the heavens raine Odours on you.	
90	Andrew	That youth's a rare Courtier, raine odours,[1] wel.	
	Viola	My matter hath no voice Lady, but to your owne most pregnant and vouchsafed eare.	L 273[2] - b
	Andrew	Odours, pregnant, and vouchsafed : [3] Ile get 'em all three already. [4]	
95	Olivia	Let the Garden doore be shut, and leave mee to my hearing. [5]	
		Give me your hand sir.	
	Viola	My dutie Madam, and most humble service [6]	
	Olivia	What is your name?	
100	Viola	Cesario is your servants name, faire Princesse.	
	Olivia	My servant sir?	
		'Twas never merry world,	
		Since lowly feigning was call'd complement :	
		[7] y'are servant to the Count Orsino youth.	

PCT [1] since Andrew is quoting Viola, most modern texts put the phrase within quotation marks

COMP [2] here the F1 page number is out of sequence: if numbered logically the column would be L265, not L273

PCT [3] see fn. #1 above

W [4] though most modern texts agree with Ff and print this as 'already', one gloss = 'all ready'

SD [5] most modern texts add an exit for Toby, Andrew, and Maria

PCT [6] F2/most modern texts = a period: F1's blurred setting could be a '?', (used as an exclamation point)

COMP/VP [7] as with several of the plays set in the later part of the Comedy section (including *As You Like It* and *Alls Well that Ends Well*), several verse lines starting with the letter 'y' are set with a lowercase letter ('y'are') instead of an uppercase one ('Y'are'): the cause seems to be either a lack of uppercase letters, or uneasy mix of lower and uppercase letters in the compositor's type tray: rarely does the setting mean the line is prose rather than verse: F2/most modern texts set uppercase letters for the last two examples, F3/most modern texts set uppercase letters for this and the one following

105	**Viola**	And he is yours, and his must needs be yours : your servants servant, is your servant Madam.
	Olivia	For him, I thinke not on him : for his thoughts, Would they were blankes, rather then fill'd with me.
110	**Viola**	Madam, I come to whet your gentle thoughts On his behalfe.
	Olivia	O by your leave I pray you. I bad you never speake againe of him ; But would you undertake another suite I had rather heare you, to solicit that,
115		Then Musicke from the spheares.
	Viola	Deere Lady. [1]
	Olivia	Give me leave, beseech you : I did send, After the last enchantment you did heare, A Ring in chace of you.
120		So did I abuse My selfe, my servant, and I feare me you : Under your hard construction must I sit, To force that on you in a shamefull cunning Which you knew none of yours.
125		What might you think? Have you not set mine Honor at the stake, And baited it with all th'unmuzled thoughts That tyrannous heart can think?
		To one of your receiving
130		Enough is shewne, a Cipresse, not a bosome, Hides my [2] heart : so let me heare you speake.
	Viola	I pittie you.
	Olivia	That's a degree to love.
	Viola	No not a grize : for tis a vulgar proofe
135		That verie oft we pitty enemies.
	Olivia	Why then me thinkes 'tis time to smile agen : O world, how apt the poore are to be proud?

[1] some modern texts replace the period of Ff with a dash, suggesting Olivia interrupts Viola

[2] most modern texts follow F1 and set this as a nine syllable line: a few follow F2 and create pentameter by adding 'poore', thus removing Olivia's (potential) hesitation before her final phrase

54

If one should be a prey, how much the better
To fall before the Lion, then the Wolfe?

CLOCKE STRIKES [1]

140 The clocke upbraides me with the waste of time :
Be not affraid good youth, I will not have you,
And yet when wit and youth is come to harvest,
[2] your wife is like to reape a proper man :
There lies your way, due West.

145 **Viola** Then Westward hoe :
Grace and good disposition attend your Ladyship :
you'l [3] nothing Madam to my Lord, by me :

Olivia Stay : I prethee tell me what thou thinkst of me? [4]

Viola That you do thinke you are not what you are.

150 **Olivia** If I thinke so, I thinke the same of you.

Viola Then thinke you right : I am not what I am.

Olivia I would you were, as I would have you be.

Viola Would it be better Madam, then I am?

I wish it might, for now I am your foole.

155 **Olivia** [5] O what a deale of scorne, lookes beautifull? [6]
In the contempt and anger of his lip,
A murdrous guilt shewes not it selfe more soone,
Then love that would seeme hid : Loves night, is noone.

R 273* - b : 3. 1. 128 - 148

[UE]1 normally such a stage direction would be set alongside the text, thus indicating that it should occur
concurrently with the stage action: this unusual placing for it (centered on a separate line) would seem to
suggest that all the stage action stops until the clock finishes striking

[W]2 F1 = 'your', F2 and most modern texts = 'Your' (see footnote #7, page 53)

[W]3 F1 = 'you'l', F2 and most modern texts = 'You'l' (again, see footnote #7, page 53)

[LS]4 Ff set an eleven syllable line as shown: some modern texts set 'Stay' as a separate line

[A]5 most modern texts indicate the following four lines are spoken as an aside

[PCT]6 most modern texts remove both pieces of punctuation from this line, and add it to the next line to form a
two line sentence, viz.

O what a deale of scorne lookes beautifull
In the contempt and anger of his lip!

however, F1 - 3's original setting allows for much more fluster from the truly besotted Olivia, viz.

O what a deale of scorne, lookes beautifull?
In the contempt and anger of his lip,/A murdrous guilt . . .

(F4 maintains F1-3's question mark at the end of the first line, and sets the (new) exclamation point at the
end of the second)

55

160   Cesario, by the Roses of the Spring,
                     By maid-hood, honor, truth, and every thing,   R 273[1] - b
                     I love thee so, that maugre all thy pride,
                     Nor wit, nor reason, can my passion hide:
                     Do not extort thy reasons from this clause,
                     For that I woo, thou therefore hast no cause:
165   But rather reason thus, with reason fetter;
                     Love sought, is good: but given unsought, is better.

       Viola   By innocence I sweare, and by my youth,
                     I have one heart, one bosome, and one truth,
                     And that no woman has, nor never none
170   Shall mistris be of it, save I alone.

                     And so adieu good Madam, never more,
                     Will I my Masters teares to you deplore.

       Olivia   Yet come againe: for thou perhaps mayst move
                     That heart which now abhorres, to like his love.

                           [Exeunt]

COMP [1] here the F1 page number is out of sequence: if numbered logically the column would be R265, not R273

Scœna Secunda

ENTER SIR TOBY, SIR ANDREW, AND FABIAN

	Andrew	No faith, Ile not stay a jot longer: [1]
	Toby	Thy reason deere venom, give thy reason.
	Fabian	You must needes yeelde your reason, Sir An- drew?
5	**Andrew**	Marry I saw your Neece do more favours to the Counts Serving-man, then ever she bestow'd upon mee: I saw't i'th Orchard.
	Toby	Did she see [2] the while, old boy, tell me that.
	Andrew	As plaine as I see you now.
10	**Fabian**	This was a great argument of love in her toward you.
	Andrew	S'light; will you make an Asse o'me.
	Fabian	I will prove it legitimate sir, upon the Oathes of judgement, and reason.
15	**Toby**	And they have beene grand Jurie men, since before Noah was a Saylor.
	Fabian	Shee did shew favour to the youth in your sight, onely to exasperate you, to awake your dormouse valour, to put fire in your Heart, and brimstone in your Liver: you should then have accosted her, and with some excel- lent jests, fire-new from the mint, you should have bangd the youth into dumbenesse: this was look'd for at your hand, and this was baulkt: the double gilt of this oppor- tunitie you let time wash off, and you are now sayld into the North of my Ladies opinion, where you will hang like an ysickle on a Dutchmans beard, unlesse you do re- deeme it, by some laudable attempt, either of valour or policie.
20		
25		

PCT [1] F1 - 2 set a colon at the end of the line, suggesting Toby (horrified at losing his drinking ticket?) perhaps interrupts Andrew: F3/most modern texts set a period

W [2] most modern texts follow F3 and set 'thee', F1 - 2 omit the word

30	**Andrew**	And't be any way, it must be with Valour, for policie I hate: I had as liefe be a Brownist, as a Politi- cian.
	Toby	Why then build me thy fortunes upon the basis of valour.

Toby (continued)

Challenge me the Counts youth to fight with him [1]
hurt him in eleven places, my Neece shall take note of it,
and assure thy selfe, there is no love-Broker in the world,
can more prevaile in mans commendation with woman,
then report of valour.

Fabian There is no way but this sir Andrew.

Andrew Will either of you beare me a challenge to him?

Toby Go, write it in a martial hand, be curst and briefe:
it is no matter how wittie, so it bee eloquent, and full of
invention: taunt him with the license of Inke: if thou
thou'st him some thrice, it shall not be amisse, and as many Lyes, as will lye in thy sheete of paper, although the
sheete were bigge enough for the bedde of Ware in Eng- L 266 - b
land, set 'em downe, go about it.

Let there bee gaulle e-
nough in thy inke, though thou write with a Goose-pen,
no matter: about it.

Andrew Where shall I finde you?

Toby Wee'l call thee at the Cubiculo: Go.

[Exit Sir Andrew]

Fabian This is a deere Manakin to you Sir Toby.

Toby I have beene deere to him lad, some two thousand
strong, or so.

Fabian We shall have a rare Letter from him; but you'le
not deliver't.

Toby Never trust me then: and by all meanes stirre on
the youth to an answer.

I thinke Oxen and waine-ropes
cannot hale them together.

For Andrew, if he were open'd
and you finde so much blood in his Liver, as will clog the
foote of a flea, Ile eate the rest of th'anatomy.

[PCT] [1] F1 - 2 set no punctuation as if Toby's imagination runs away with him: F3/most modern texts set a
comma

65	**Fabian**	And his opposit the youth beares in his visage no great presage of cruelty.

ENTER MARIA

	Toby	Looke where the youngest Wren of mine [1] comes.
70	**Maria**	If you desire the spleene, and will laughe your selves into stitches, follow me; yond gull Malvolio is tur-ned Heathen, a verie Renegatho; for there is no christian that meanes to be saved by beleeving rightly, can ever beleeve such impossible passages of grossenesse.

Hee's in

yellow stockings.

75	**Toby**	And crosse garter'd?
	Maria	Most villanously: like a Pedant that keepes a Schoole i'th Church: I have dogg'd him like his murthe-rer.

He does obey every point of the Letter that I dropt,
to betray him: He does smile his face into more lynes,
then is in the new mappe, with the augmentation of the
Indies: you have not seene such a thing as tis: I can hardly forbeare hurling things at him, I know my Ladie will
strike him: if shee doe, hee'l smile, and take't for a great
favour.

	Toby	Come bring us, bring us where he is.

[Exeunt Omnes]

[W] [1] some modern texts = 'nine', Ff = 'mine'

Scæna Tertia

ENTER SEBASTIAN AND ANTHONIO [1]

Sebastian	I would not by my will have troubled you, [†2]
	But since you make your pleasure of your paines,
	I will no further chide you.
Antonio	I could not stay behinde you : my desire
	(More sharpe then filed steele) did spurre me forth,
	And not all love to see you (though so much
	As might have drawne one to a longer voyage)
	But jealousie, what might befall your travell, [†3]
	Being skillesse in these parts : which to a stranger,
	Unguided, and unfriended, often prove
	Rough, and unhospitable.
	My willing love,
	The rather by these arguments of feare
	Set forth in your pursuite.

5

10

}

Sebastian	My kinde Anthonio,
	I can no other answer make, but thankes,
	And thankes : and ever [4] oft good turnes,
	Are shuffel'd off with such uncurrant pay :
	But were my worth, as is my conscience firme,
	You should finde better dealing : what's to do?
	Shall we go see the reliques of this Towne?

15

20

R 266 - b

Antonio	To morrow sir, best first go see your Lodging?
Sebastian	I am not weary, and 'tis long to night [5]
	I pray you let us satisfie our eyes
	With the memorials, and the things of fame
	That do renowne this City.

25

[N/P 1] though the play is supposedly set by a single compositor throughout (Compositor B) the character previously spelled as 'Antonio' in both stage direction and dialogue is now set as 'Anthonio' for the rest of the play: the prefix used in this text will remain as shown at his first entry ('Antonio'), but wherever he is referred to by name within the dialogue, whatever setting F1 uses (nearly always 'Anthonio') will be followed

[W 2] F1 = 'yo u', F2/most modern texts = 'you'

[W 3] F2 and most modern texts = 'travell', F1 = 'rravell'

[W 4] most modern texts = 'And thanks, and ever thanks; and oft . . .', Ff = 'And thankes: and ever oft . . .'

[PCT 5] F1 sets no punctuation, as if Sebastian's eagerness is getting the better of him: F2 sets a comma, most modern texts a period

Antonio	Would you'd pardon me: ﹜	
	I do not without danger walke these streetes.	
	Once in a sea-fight 'gainst the Count his gallies,	
30	I did some service, of such note indeede,	
	That were I tane heere, it would scarse be answer'd.	
Sebastian	Belike you slew great number of his people. [1]	
Antonio	Th'offence[†2] is not of such a bloody nature,	
	Albeit the quality of the time, and quarrell	
35	Might well have given us bloody argument:	
	It might have since bene answer'd in repaying	
	What we tooke from them, which for Traffiques sake	
	Most of our City did.	
	Onely my selfe stood out,	
40	For which if I be lapsed [3] in this place	
	I shall pay deere.	
Sebastian	Do not then walke too open. ﹜	
Antonio	It doth not fit me: hold sir, here's my purse,	
	In the South Suburbes at the Elephant	
45	Is best to lodge: I will bespeake our dyet,	
	Whiles you beguile the time, and feed your knowledge	
	With viewing of the Towne, there shall you have me.	
Sebastian	Why I your purse?	
Antonio	Haply your eye shall light upon some toy	
50	You have desire to purchase: and your store	
	I thinke is not for idle Markets, sir.	
Sebastian	Ile be your purse-bearer, and leave you	
	For an houre.	
Antonio	To th'Elephant. ﹜	
55 **Sebastian**	I do remember.	

[Exeunt]

[PCT][1] most modern texts set the grammatically correct question mark: however, the Ff period is of good theatrical merit, for if it were spoken as a simple statement of fact it would suggest a beautifully naive assumption about Anthonio's derring-do by Sebastian

[W][2] F1 = 'Th offence', F2/most modern texts = 'Th'offence'

[W][3] though most modern texts agree with Ff and set 'lapsed', one gloss = 'latched'

Scœna Quarta

ENTER OLIVIA AND MARIA [1]

Olivia	I have sent after him, he sayes hee'l come:
	How shall I feast him?
	What bestow of him?
	For youth is bought more oft, then begg'd, or borrow'd.

5

I speake too loud: [2] Where's Malvolio, he is sad, and civill,
And suites well for a servant with my fortunes,
Where is Malvolio?

}

Maria	[3] He's comming Madame:
	But in very strange manner.
	He is sure possest Madam.

10

Olivia	Why what's the matter, does he rave?
Maria	No Madam, he does nothing but smile: your La-
	dyship were best to have some guard about you, if hee
	come, for sure the man is tainted in's wits.

15

Olivia	Go call him hither. [4]

ENTER MALVOLIO

I am as madde as hee,
If sad and merry [†5] madnesse equall bee.

How now Malvolio?

}

Malvolio	Sweet Lady, ho, ho.

SD/A [1] most modern texts suggest that Maria is following, or at a distance, so that Olivia opens with an aside

LS [2] though Ff set this as a 14 syllable line thus allowing Olivia her overwrought confusion, most modern texts start a new line after this point, thus giving the chance to gain self-control (by creating a short line followed by a normal line of pentameter)

VP [3] most modern texts now set the scene in prose, though Ff seem to suggest the appearance of formality is maintained until Maria starts to reply to Olivia's question as to Malvolio's madness

SD [4] most modern texts suggest Maria exits, and that Malvolio's entry is delayed for a line and a half: this does create order within the scene, but the Ff setting allows for the mayhem to start here, with Maria staying on-stage to witness Malvolio's early entry (does he pose for effect?) and Olivia's talking to herself

W [5] F1 = 'metry', F2/most modern texts = 'merry'

62

20	**Olivia**	Smil'st thou?

                                        I sent for thee upon a sad occasion.

	Malvolio	[1] Sad Lady, I could be sad:

This does make some obstruction in the blood:

This crosse-gartering, but what of that?   L 267 - b

25   If it please the eye of one, it is with me as the very true

Sonnet is: Please one, and please all.

	{Malvolio} [2]	Why how doest thou man?

What is the matter with thee?

	Malvolio	Not blacke in my minde, though yellow in my

30   legges: It did come to his hands, and Commaunds shall

be executed.

                            I thinke we doe know the sweet Romane

hand.

	Olivia	Wilt thou go to bed Malvolio?

35	**Malvolio**	To bed?

                      I sweet heart, and Ile come to thee.

	Olivia	God comfort thee: Why dost thou smile so, and

kisse thy hand so oft?

	Maria	How do you Malvolio?

40	**Malvolio**	At your request: → [3]

Yes Nightingales answere Dawes.

	Maria	Why appeare you with this ridiculous bold-

nesse before my Lady.

	Malvolio	[4] Be not afraid of greatnesse: 'twas well writ.

45	**Olivia**	What meanst thou by that Malvolio?

[LS][1] Ff set the opening of this speech as slightly irregular verse (7/10/8 or 9 syllables) as if Malvolio were struggling to maintain composure: arguing white space, most modern texts set it as prose

[P][2] F2 and most modern texts assign this to Olivia, F1 to Malvolio

[VP][3] if Malvolio's lines are verse, then this Ff single split line offers him a wonderful moment as he pauses to consider whether to answer Maria or no

[VP][4] there is the possibility that all Malvolio's lines in the following sequence may be in verse; (including the split line with Olivia the syllable count would be 10/10/9/12/8/12/10): this would certainly add credence to his 'frenzy', especially if Olivia is frightened into prose - the contrast between them would be enormous

	Malvolio	Some are borne great. [1] *
	Olivia	Ha?
	Malvolio	Some atcheeve greatnesse. *
	Olivia	What sayest thou?
50	**Malvolio**	And some have greatnesse thrust upon them.
	Olivia	Heaven restore thee.
	Malvolio	Remember who commended thy yellow stock- ings. *
	Olivia	Thy yellow stockings?
55	**Malvolio**	And wish'd to see thee crosse garter'd. *
	Olivia	Crosse garter'd?
	Malvolio	Go too, thou art made, if thou desir'st to be so.
	Olivia	Am I made?
	Malvolio	If not, let[2] me see thee a servant still.
60	**Olivia**	Why this is verie Midsommer madnesse.

ENTER SERVANT

	Servant	Madame, the young Gentleman of the Count Orsino's is return'd, I could hardly entreate him backe: he attends your Ladyships pleasure.
	Olivia	Ile come to him. [3]
65		Good Maria, let this fellow be look'd[4] too.

Where's my
Cosine Toby, let some of my people have a speciall care
of him, I would not have him miscarrie for the halfe of
my Dowry.

[exit]

R 267 - b : 3. 4. 41 - 63

[PCT 1] some modern texts replace the period of Ff with a dash, suggesting Malvolio's excitement continues, so that Olivia's lines are interruptions to which he pays little or no attention: all similar modern text resettings in this scene will be marked with the symbol * without an accompanying footnote

[W 2] F2 and most modern texts = 'let', F1 = 'ler'

[SD 3] most modern texts add a stage direction here for the Servant to exit

[W 4] F1 = 'look d', F2/most modern texts = 'look'd'

| 70 | **Malvolio** | Oh ho, do you come neere me now: no worse man then sir Toby to looke to me. |

This concurres direct-
ly with the Letter, she sends him on purpose, that I may
appeare stubborne to him: for she incites me to that in
75 the Letter.

Cast thy humble slough sayes she: be opposite with a Kinsman, surly with servants, let thy tongue
langer [1] with arguments of state, put thy selfe into the
tricke of singularity: and consequently setts downe the
80 manner how: as a sad face, a reverend carriage, a slow
tongue, in the habite of some Sir of note, and so foorth.

I have lymde her, but it is Joves doing, and Jove make me
thankefull.

And when she went away now, let this Fel-
85 low be look'd too: Fellow? not Malvolio, nor after my
degree, but Fellow.

Why every thing adheres togither,
that no dramme of a scruple, no scruple of a scruple, no
obstacle, no incredulous or unsafe circumstance: What
90 can be saide?

Nothing that can be, can come betweene
me, and the full prospect of my hopes.

Well Jove, not I,
is the doer of this, and he is to be thanked.

ENTER TOBY, FABIAN, AND MARIA

R 267 - b

| 95 | **Toby** | Which way is hee in the name of sanctity. |

If all
the divels of hell be drawne in little, and Legion himselfe
possest him, yet Ile speake to him.

| | **Fabian** | Heere he is, heere he is: how ist with you sir? |
| 100 | | How ist with you man? [2] |

| | **Malvolio** | Go off, I discard you: let me enjoy my private: go off. |

| | **Maria** | Lo, how hollow the fiend speakes within him; did not I tell you? |

105

Sir Toby, my Lady prayes you to have
a care of him.

R 267 - b / L 268 - b : 3. 4. 64 - 93

[W] [1] F1 = 'langer', F2 and most modern texts = 'tang'

[P] [2] since Fabian uses 'sir' to Malvolio, most modern texts assign this second sentence (using 'man') to Toby

	Malvolio	Ah ha, does she so?
	Toby	Go too, go too : peace, peace, wee must deale
		gently with him : Let me alone.
110		How do you Malvolio?
		How ist with you?
		What man, defie the divell : consider,
		he's an enemy to mankinde.
	Malvolio	Do you know what you say?
115	**Maria**	La you, and you speake ill of the divell, how
		he takes it at heart [1] Pray God he be not bewitch'd.
	Fabian	Carry his water to th'wise woman.
	Maria	Marry and it shall be done to morrow morning
		if I live.
120		My Lady would not loose him for more then ile
		say.
	Malvolio	How now mistris?
	Maria	Oh Lord.
	Toby	Prethee hold thy peace, this is not the way : Doe
125		you not see you move him?
		Let me alone with him.
	Fabian	No way but gentlenesse, gently, gently : the Fiend
		is rough, and will not be roughly us'd.
	Toby	Why how now my bawcock? how dost ÿ [2] chuck?
130	**Malvolio**	Sir.
	Toby	I biddy, come with me.
		What man, tis not for
		gravity to play at cherrie-pit with fathan [3] Hang him foul
		Colliar.
135	**Maria**	Get him to say his prayers, good sir Toby gette
		him to pray.

PCT 1 in F1 there is a gap where a period could have been set and fallen out of the tray: F2 and most modern texts set the period

AB 2 F1 = 'ÿ', (printed as such because of lack of column width), F2/most modern texts = 'thou'

PCT 3 in F1 there is a gap where a period could have been set and fallen out of the tray: F2 and most modern texts set the period

	Malvolio	My prayers Minx.
	Maria	No I warrant you, he will not heare of godly-nesse.
140	**Malvolio**	Go hang your selves all : you are ydle shallowe things, I am not of your element, you shall knowe more heereafter.

[Exit]

	Toby	Ist possible?
145	**Fabian**	If this were plaid upon a stage now, I could con-demne it as an improbable fiction.
	Toby	His very genius hath taken the infection of the device man.
	Maria	Nay pursue him now, least the device take ayre, and taint.
150	**Fabian**	Why we shall make him mad indeede.
	Maria	The house will be the quieter.
	Toby	Come, wee'l have him in a darke room & bound.
155		My Neece is already in the beleefe that he's mad : we may carry it thus for our pleasure, and his pennance, til our ve-ry pastime tyred out of breath, prompt us to have mercy on him : at which time, we will bring the device to the bar and crowne thee for a finder of madmen : but see, but see.

ENTER SIR ANDREW

	Fabian	More matter for a May morning.
160	**Andrew**	Heere's the Challenge, reade it : I warrant there's vinegar and pepper in't.
	Fabian	Ist so sawcy?
	Andrew	I, ist? I warrant him : do but read.
	Toby	Give me.
165		[1] *Youth, whatsoever thou art, thou art but a scurvy fellow.*

L 268 - b   :   3. 4. 120 - 148

[SD][1] most modern texts indicate Toby starts to read the letter: this script will follow Ff and usually set the 'letter text' in italics, thus avoiding the need to keep repeating the footnote 'read'

Fabian	Good, and valiant.	
Toby	*Wonder not, nor admire not in thy minde why I doe call*	L 268 - b
	thee so, for I will shew thee no reason for't.	
Fabian	A good note, that keepes you from the blow of ÿ [1] Law[†]	

170 **Toby**   *Thou comst to the Lady Olivia, and in my sight she uses*
                       thee kindly : but thou lyest in thy throat, that is not the matter
                       I challenge thee for .

      Fabian   Very breefe, and to exceeding good sence-lesse.

      Toby   *I will way-lay thee going home, where if it be thy chance*
175   *to kill me .*

      Fabian   Good.

      Toby   *Thou kilst me like a rogue and a villaine .*

      Fabian   Still you keepe o'th windie side of the Law : good.

      Toby   *Fartheewell, and God have mercie upon one of our*
180   *soules .*
                              He may have mercie upon mine, but my hope is better,
                       and so looke to thy selfe .
                                  Thy friend as thou usest him, & thy
                       sworne enemie, Andrew Ague-cheeke .

185   **Toby**   If this Letter move him not, his legges cannot :
                       Ile giv't him.

      Maria   You[†2] may have verie fit occasion for't[†] : [3] he is now
                       in some commerce with my Ladie, and will by and by
                       depart.

190   **Toby**   Go sir Andrew : scout mee for him at the corner
                       of the Orchard like a bum-Baylie : so soone as ever thou
                       seest him, draw, and as thou draw'st, sweare horrible : for
                       it[†4] comes to passe oft, that a terrible oath, with a swagge-
                       ring accent sharpely twang'd off, gives manhoode more
195   approbation, then ever proofe it selfe would have earn'd
                       him.
                       Away.

L 268 - b / R 268 - b : 3. 4. 149 - 182

[AB][1] F1 = 'ÿ', (printed as such because of lack of column width), F2/most modern texts = 'the'

[▼][2] F2 and most modern texts = 'You', F1 = 'Yon'

[▼][3] F2 and most modern texts = 'for't', F1 = 'fot't'

[▼][4] F2 and most modern texts = 'it', F1 sets a blurred mark and 't'

Andrew	Nay let me alone for swearing.

[Exit]

Toby	Now will not I deliver his Letter: for the behavi-

200 our of the yong Gentleman, gives him out to be of good
capacity, and breeding: his employment betweene his
Lord and my Neece, confirmes no lesse.

> Therefore, this
Letter being so excellently ignorant, will breed no terror
205 in the youth: he will finde it comes from a Clodde-pole.

But sir, I will deliver his Challenge by word of mouth;
set upon Ague-cheeke a notable report of valor, and drive
the Gentleman (as I know his youth will aptly receive it)
into a most hideous opinion of his rage, skill, furie, and
210 impetuositie.

> This will so fright them both, that they wil
kill one another by the looke, like Cockatrices.

ENTER OLIVIA AND VIOLA [1]

Fabian	Heere he comes with your Neece, give them way

till he take leave, and presently after him.

215 **Toby**	I wil meditate the while upon some horrid message

for a Challenge. [2]

Olivia	I have said too much unto a hart of stone,

And laid mine honour too unchary on't: [3]
There's something in me that reproves my fault:
220 But such a head-strong potent fault it is,
That it but mockes reproofe.

Viola	With the same haviour that your passion beares,

Goes on my Masters greefes.

Olivia	Heere, weare this Jewell for me, tis my picture:

225 Refuse it not, it hath no tongue, to vex you:
And I beseech you come againe to morrow.

What shall you aske of me that Ile deny,
That honour (sav'd) may upon asking give.

Viola	Nothing but this, your true love for my master.

---

[1] most modern texts delay the entry until after Fabian's speech

[2] most modern texts add a stage direction here for the exit of Toby, Fabian, and Maria

[3] though most modern texts agree with Ff and print this as 'on't', one gloss = 'out'

230	**Olivia**	How with mine honor may I give him that,
		Which I have given to you.
		}
	Viola	I will acquit you.
	Olivia	Well, come againe to morrow: far-thee-well,
		A Fiend like thee might beare my soule to hell. [1]

ENTER TOBY AND FABIAN

235	**Toby**	Gentleman, God save thee.	R 268 - b
	Viola	And you sir.
	Toby	That defence thou hast, betake the [2] too't: of what
		nature the wrongs are thou hast done him, I knowe not:
		but thy intercepter full of despight, bloody as the Hun-
240		ter, attends thee at the Orchard end: dismount thy tucke,
		be yare in thy preparation, for thy assaylant is quick, skil-
		full, and deadly.
	Viola	You mistake sir I am sure, no man hath any quar-
		rell to me: my remembrance is very free and cleere from
245		any image of offence done to any man.
	Toby	You'l finde it otherwise I assure you: therefore, if
		you hold your life at any price, betake you to your gard:
		for your opposite hath in him what youth, strength, skill,
		and wrath, can furnish man withall.
250	**Viola**	I pray you sir what is he?
	Toby	He is knight dubb'd with unhatch'd Rapier, and
		on carpet consideration, but he is a divell in private brall,
		soules and bodies hath he divorc'd three, and his incense-
		ment at this moment is so implacable, that satisfaction
255		can be none, but by pangs of death and sepulcher: Hob,
		nob, is his word: giv't or take't.
	Viola	I will returne againe into the house, and desire
		some conduct of the Lady.
		I am no fighter, I have heard
260		of some kinde of men, that put quarrells purposely on o-
		thers, to taste their valour: belike this is a man of that
		quirke.

[SD] [1] most modern texts add a stage direction here for Olivia to exit

[W] [2] F1 = 'the', F2 and most modern texts = 'thee'

Toby	Sir, no: his indignation derives it selfe out of a ve-
	ry computent [1] injurie, therefore get you on, and give him
265	his desire.
	Backe you shall not to the house, unlesse you
	undertake that with me, which with as much safetie you
	might answer him: therefore on, or strippe your sword
	starke naked: for meddle you must that's certain, or for-
270	sweare to weare iron about you.
Viola	This is as uncivill as strange.
	I beseech you, doe
	me this courteous office, as to know of the Knight what
	my offence to him is: it is something of my negligence,
275	nothing of my purpose.
Toby	I will doe so.
	Signiour Fabian, stay you by this
	Gentleman, till my returne.

[Exit Toby]

Viola	Pray you sir, do you know of this matter?
280 **Fabian**	I know the knight is incenst against you, even to
	a mortall arbitrement, but nothing of the circumstance
	more.
Viola	I beseech you what manner of man is he?
Fabian	Nothing of that wonderfull promise to read him
285	by his forme, as you are like to finde him in the proofe of
	his valour.
	He is indeede sir, the most skilfull, bloudy, &
	fatall opposite that you could possibly have found in anie
	part of Illyria: will you walke towards him, I will make
290	your peace with him, if I can.
Viola	I shall bee much bound to you for't: I am one,
	that had rather go with sir Priest, then sir knight: I care
	not who knowes so much of my mettle.

[Exeunt]
ENTER TOBY AND ANDREW

---

[1] F1 - 3 = 'computent', F4 and some modern texts = 'competent'

Toby	Why man hee's[1] a verie divell, I have not seen such	
295	a firago: I had a passe with him, rapier, scabberd, and all:	
	and he gives me the stucke in with such a mortall motion	
	that it is inevitable: and on the answer, he payes you as	
	surely, as your feete hits[2] the ground they step on.	
	They	
300	say, he has bin Fencer to the Sophy.	

Andrew Pox on't, Ile not meddle with him.

Toby I but he will not now be pacified,
Fabian can scarse hold him yonder. [3]

Andrew Plague on't, and I thought he had beene valiant,
305 and so cunning in Fence, I'de have seene him damn'd ere
I'de have challeng'd him.

Let him let the matter slip, and   L 269 - b
Ile give him my horse, gray Capilet.

Toby Ile make the motion: stand heere, make a good
310 shew on't, this shall end without the perdition of soules,
[4] marry Ile ride your horse as well as I ride you.

ENTER FABIAN AND VIOLA

[5] I have his horse to take up the quarrell, I have perswaded
him the youths a divell.

Fabian He is as horribly conceited of him: and pants, &
315 lookes pale, as if a Beare were at his heeles.

Toby There's no remedie sir, he will fight with you for's
oath sake: marrie hee hath better bethought him of his
quarrell, and hee findes that now scarse to bee worth talking of: therefore draw for the supportance of his vowe,
320 he protests he will not hurt you.

Viola [6] Pray God defend me: a little thing would make
me tell them how much I lacke of a man.

W 1 F1 = 'hee s', F2 and most modern texts = 'he's'

W 2 some modern texts = 'hit', Ff = 'hits'

VP 3 Ff seem to set this 'grim' news from Toby as verse (10/8 or 9 syllables): arguing 'white space' created the
need for an extra line to fill up the column, most modern texts set the speech as prose

A 4 most modern texts indicate the remainder of this speech is spoken as an aside

A 5 most modern texts indicate this sentence and the reply are spoken as asides between Toby and Fabian
before Toby turns his attentions to Viola once more

A 6 most modern texts indicate this is spoken as an aside

	Fabian	Give ground if you see him furious.
325	**Toby**	Come sir Andrew, there's no remedie, the Gen-tleman will for his honors sake have one bowt with you: he cannot by the Duello avoide it: but hee has promised me, as he is a Gentleman and a Soldiour, he will not hurt you.
		Come on, too't.
330	**Andrew**	Pray God he keepe his oath.

ENTER ANTONIO [1]

	Viola	I do assure you tis against my will.
	Antonio	Put up your sword: if this yong Gentleman Have done offence, I take the fault on me: If you offend him, I for him defie you.
335	**Toby**	You sir?
		Why, what are you?
	Antonio	One sir, that for his love dares yet do more Then you have heard him brag to you he will.
	Toby	Nay, if you be an undertaker, I am for you. [2]

ENTER OFFICERS

340	**Fabian**	O good sir Toby hold: heere come the Officers.
	Toby	Ile be with you anon. [3]
	Viola	Pray sir, put your sword up if you please.
	Andrew	Marry will I sir: and for that I promis'd you Ile be as good as my word.
345		Hee will beare you easily, and raines well.
	1st Officer	This is the man, do thy Office.
	2nd Officer	Anthonio, I arrest thee at the suit of Count Orsino [4]

SD [1] most modern texts place the entry one line later, and suggest Anthonio draws his sword immediately, though it seems possible that he could draw his sword at any time up to the point Toby agrees to fight

SD [2] most modern texts add a stage direction for Toby to draw his sword

WHO [3] most modern texts suggest Toby's line is spoken to Anthonio, and Viola's to Andrew

PCT [4] F1 shows no punctuation at the end of the line, perhaps suggesting Anthonio interrupts the 2nd. Officer: F2 and modern texts add a period

	Andrew	You do mistake me sir.
350	**1st Officer**	No sir, no jot: I know your favour well:
		Though now you have no sea-cap on your head:
		Take him away, he knowes I know him well.
	Antonio	I must obey.

¹ This comes with seeking you:

355   But there's no remedie, I shall answer it:
What will you do: now my necessitie
Makes me to aske you for my purse.

          It greeves mee
Much more, for what I cannot do for you,
360   Then what befals my selfe: you stand amaz'd,
But be of comfort.

2nd Officer Come sir away.

Antonio I must entreat of you some of that money.

Viola What money sir?

365   For the fayre kindnesse you have shew'd me heere,
And part being prompted by your present trouble,
Out of my leane and low ability
Ile lend you something: my having is not much,
Ile make division of my present with you:
370   Hold, there's halfe my Coffer.

Antonio Will you deny me now,
Ist possible that my deserts to you
Can lacke perswasion.

        Do not tempt my misery,
375   Least that it make me so unsound a man
As to upbraid you with those kindnesses   R 269 - b
That I have done for you.

Viola I know of none,
Nor know I you by voyce, or any feature:
380   I hate ingratitude more in a man,
Then lying, vainnesse, babling drunkennesse,
Or any taint of vice, whose strong corruption
Inhabites our fraile blood.

Antonio Oh heavens themselves.

385 **2nd Officer** Come sir, I pray you go. ²

WHO ¹ most modern texts indicate this is spoken to Viola

SP ² the actor has choice as to which two of these three short lines may be joined as one line of split verse

	Antonio	Let me speake a little.
		This youth that you see heere,[†]
		I snatch'd one halfe out of the jawes of death,
		Releev'd him with such sanctitie of love;
390		And to his image, which me thought did promise
		Most venerable worth, did I devotion.
	1st Officer	What's that to us, the time goes by: Away.
	Antonio	But oh, how vilde an idoll proves this God:
		Thou hast Sebastian done good feature, shame.
395		In Nature, there's no blemish but the minde:
		None can be call'd deform'd, but the unkinde.
		Vertue is beauty, but the beauteous evill
		Are empty trunkes, ore-flourish'd by the devill.
	1st Officer	The man growes mad, away with him: → [1]
400		Come, come sir.
	Antonio	Leade me on.

[Exit]

	Viola	Me thinkes his words do from such passion flye
		That he beleeves himselfe, so do not I:
		Prove true imagination, oh prove true,[†2]
405		That I deere brother, be now tane for you.
	Toby	Come hither Knight, come hither Fabian: Weel
		whisper ore a couplet or two of most sage sawes.
	Viola	He nam'd Sebastian: I my brother know
		Yet living in my glasse: even such, and so
410		In favour was my Brother, and he went
		Still in this fashion, colour, ornament,
		For him I imitate: Oh if it prove,
		Tempests are kinde, and salt waves fresh in love. [3]
	Toby	A very dishonest paltry boy, and more a coward
415		then a Hare, his dishonesty appeares, in leaving his frend
		heere in necessity, and denying him: and for his coward-
		ship aske Fabian.

[VP]1 these two short Ff lines (8/3 syllables) are set as a single verse line in most modern texts: the F1 setting allows gaps for the seizure of/struggle by Anthonio

[W]2 F2 and most modern texts = 'true', F1 = 'ttue'

[SD]3 most modern texts add a stage direction for Viola's exit

Fabian		A Coward, a most devout Coward, religious in it.
420	**Andrew**	Slid Ile after him againe, and beate him.
	Toby	Do, cuffe him soundly, but never draw thy sword [1]
	Andrew	And I do not. [2]
	Fabian	Come, let's see the event.
	Toby	I dare lay any money, twill be nothing yet.

[Exit]

L 270 - b : 3. 4. 389 - 396

---

[1] PCT F1 - 2 = no punctuation (possibly as if Andrew interrupts him), F3/most modern texts print a period

[2] SD/PCT most modern texts give Andrew an exit here, and end the sentence with a dash as if he were still talking as he leaves

Actus Quartus, Scœna prima

ENTER SEBASTIAN AND CLOWNE

	Clowne	Will you make me beleeve, that I am not sent for
		you?
	Sebastian	Go too, go too, thou art a foolish fellow,
		Let me be cleere of thee. [1]
5	**Clowne**	Well held out yfaith: No, I do not know you,
		nor I am not sent to you by my Lady, to bid you come
		speake with her: nor your name is not Master Cesario,
		nor this is not my nose neyther: Nothing that is so, is so.
	Sebastian	I prethee vent thy folly some-where else,° thou
10		know'st not me.°
	Clowne	Vent my folly: He has heard that word of some
		great man, and now applyes it to a foole.

Vent my fol-   L 270 - b
ly: I am affraid this great lubber the World will prove a
15   Cockney: I prethee now ungird thy strangenes, and tell
me what I shall vent to my Lady?
                              Shall I vent to hir that
thou art comming?

	Sebastian	I prethee foolish greeke depart from me,° there's
20		money for thee, if you tarry longer,° I shall give worse
		paiment.
	Clowne	By my troth thou hast an open hand: these Wise-
		men that give fooles money, get themselves a good re-
		port, after foureteene yeares purchase.

ENTER ANDREW, TOBY, AND FABIAN

L 270 - b / R 270 - b : 4. 1. 1 - 23

[VP] [1] according to Ff, as Sebastian attempts to deal with the Clowne's persistence, he can only maintain the
formality of verse for this first speech: however, most modern texts keep his dignity throughout by turning
the following speeches into verse too, as the symbols ° show

25	**Andrew**	Now sir, have I met you again: ther's for you.
	Sebastian	¹ Why there's for thee, and there, and there, Are all the people mad?
	Toby	Hold sir, or Ile throw your dagger ore the house.
30	**Clowne**	This will I tell my Lady straight, I would not be in some of your coats for two pence. ²
	Toby	Come on sir, hold.
35	**Andrew**	Nay let him alone, Ile go another way to worke with him: Ile have an action of Battery against him, if there be any†³ law in Illyria: though I stroke him first, yet it's no matter for that.
	Sebastian	Let go thy hand.
40	**Toby**	Come sir, I will not let you go. 　　　　　　　　　　　　Come my yong souldier put up your yron: you are well flesh'd: Come on.
	Sebastian	I will be free from thee. ⁴ 　　　　　　　What wouldst ÿ⁵ now? If thou dar'st tempt me further, draw thy sword.
45	**Toby**	What, what? 　　　　　　Nay then I must have an Ounce or two of this malapert blood from you.

ENTER OLIVIA

	Olivia	Hold Toby, on thy life I charge thee hold.
	Toby	Madam. ⁶

R 270 - b　:　4. 1. 24 - 46

ᴿᴰ₁ most modern texts suggest Sebastian, having been struck by Andrew, strikes him back: Ff also have him
returning to the (careful?) control of verse, a move denied by the modern texts (see fn. # 1, page 77)

ᴿᴰ₂ most modern texts add a stage direction for the Clowne's exit

ᵂ₃ F1 = 'a ny', F2/most modern texts = 'any'

ᴿᴰ₄ most modern texts add the stage directions that Sebastian draws his sword here, and that Toby draws his
at the end of his next speech

ᴬᴮ₅ F1 = 'ÿ', (printed as such because of lack of column width), F2/most modern texts = 'thou'

ᴿᶜᵀ₆ some modern texts replace the period of Ff with a dash, suggesting Olivia interrupts Toby

	Olivia	Will it be ever thus?
50		Ungracious wretch,

Fit for the Mountaines, and the barbarous Caves,
Where manners nere were preach'd : out of my sight.

Be not offended, deere Cesario :
Rudesbey be gone. [1]

I prethee gentle friend,

55

Let thy fayre wisedome, not thy passion sway
In this uncivill, and unjust extent
Against thy peace.

Go with me to my house,

60

And heare thou there how many fruitlesse prankes
This Ruffian hath botch'd up, that thou thereby
Mayst smile at this : Thou shalt not choose but goe :
Do not denie, beshrew his soule for mee,
He started one poore heart of mine, in thee.

65 **Sebastian** What rellish is in this?

How runs the streame?

Or I am mad, or else this is a dreame :
Let fancie still my sense in Lethe steepe,
If it be thus to dreame, still let me sleepe.

70 **Olivia** Nay come I prethee, would thoud'st be rul'd by me [2]

Sebastian Madam, I will.

Olivia O say so, and so be.

[Exeunt]

[SD 1] most modern texts add an exit for Toby, Andrew and Fabian

[PCT 2] F1 shows no punctuation at the end of the line, perhaps suggesting Sebastian interrupts Olivia: F2 and modern texts add a period

Scœna Secunda

ENTER MARIA AND CLOWNE

Maria	Nay, I prethee put on this gown, & this beard, make him beleeve thou art sir Topas the Curate, doe it quickly.

        Ile call sir Toby the whilst. [1]

5 **Clowne** Well, Ile put it on, and I will dissemble my selfe in't, and I would I were the first that ever dissembled in   R 270 - b
in [2] such a gowne.

      I am not tall enough to become the function well, nor leane enough to bee thought a good
10 Studient : but to be said an honest man and a good hous-keeper goes as fairely, as to say, a carefull man, & a great scholler.

      The Competitors enter.

ENTER TOBY [3]

Toby   Jove blesse thee M. Parson.

15 **Clowne** *Bonos dies* sir Toby : for as the old hermit of Prage
that never saw pen and inke, very wittily sayd to a Neece
of King Gorbodacke, that that is, is : so I being M. Parson,
am M. Parson ; for what is that, but that ? and is, but is ?

Toby   To him sir Topas.

20 **Clowne** What hoa, I say, Peace in this prison.

Toby   The knave counterfets well : a good knave.

[Malvolio within]

R 270 - b / L 271 - b : 4. 2. 1 - 19

[SD 1] most modern texts add a stage direction for Maria's exit

[W 2] F1 alone sets 'in in' (caused by inaccurate casting off from one page to the next), F2/modern texts = 'in'

[SD 3] since the line before the entry refers to 'Competitors' in the plural, and given that Maria has lines later in the scene (67-8) most modern texts add her to the entry with Toby

	Malvolio	Who cals there?
	Clowne	Sir Topas the Curate, who comes to visit Malvo-lio the Lunaticke.
25	**Malvolio**	Sir Topas, sir Topas, good sir Topas goe to my Ladie.
	Clowne	Out hyperbolicall fiend, how vexest thou this man? Talkest thou nothing but of Ladies?
30	**Toby**	Well said M. Parson.
	Malvolio	Sir Topas, never was man thus wronged, good sir Topas do not thinke I am mad : they have layde mee heere in hideous darknesse.
35	**Clowne**	Fye, thou dishonest Sathan : I call thee by the most modest termes, for I am one of those gentle ones, that will use the divell himselfe with curtesie : sayst thou that [1] house is darke?
	Malvolio	As hell sir Topas.
40	**Clowne**	Why it hath bay Windowes transparant as bari-cadoes, and the cleere stores [2] toward the[3] South north, are as lustrous as Ebony : and yet complainest thou of ob-struction?
	Malvolio	I am not mad sir Topas, I say to you this house is darke.
45	**Clowne**	Madman thou errest : I say there is no darknesse but ignorance, in which thou art more puzel'd then the Ægyptians in their fogge.
50	**Malvolio**	I say this house is as darke as Ignorance, thogh Ignorance were as darke as hell ; and I say there was ne-ver man thus abus'd, I am no more madde then you are, make the triall of it in any constant question.
	Clowne	What is the opinion of Pythagoras concerning Wilde-fowle?

L 271 - b : 4. 2. 20 - 51

▼ [1] most modern texts = 'the', Ff omit the word

▼ [2] most modern texts = 'clerestories', Ff = 'cleere stores'

▼ [3] F1 = 't he', F2/most modern texts = 'the'

55	**Malvolio**	That the soule of our grandam, might happily inhabite a bird.
	Clowne	What thinkst thou of his opinion?
	Malvolio	I thinke nobly of the soule, and no way aprove his opinion.
60	**Clowne**	Fare thee well : remaine thou still in darkenesse, thou shalt hold th'opinion of Pythagoras, ere I will allow of thy wits, and feare to kill a Woodcocke, lest thou dis-possesse the soule of thy grandam.
		<div align="right">Fare thee well.</div>
	Malvolio	Sir Topas, sir Topas.
65	**Toby**	My most exquisite sir Topas.
	Clowne	Nay I am for all waters.
	Maria	Thou mightst have done this without thy berd [1] and gowne, he sees thee not.
70	**Toby**	To him in thine owne voyce, and bring me word how thou findst him : I would we were well ridde of this knavery.
75		If he may bee conveniently deliver'd, I would he were, for I am now so farre in offence with my Niece, that I cannot pursue with any safety this sport [2] the uppe-shot.
		<div align="right">Come by and by to my Chamber. [3]</div>

[Exit]

L 271 - b

	Clowne	• Hey Robin, jolly Robin,° tell me how thy Lady does. °[4]
	Malvolio	Foole.
80	**Clowne**	• My Lady is unkind, perdie.

L 271 - b / R 271 - b : 4. 2. 52 - 75

[W][1] F1 = 'berd', for clarity most modern texts set F2's 'beard'

[W][2] most modern texts add 'to', Ff omit the word

[A][3] most modern texts suggest this is spoken as an aside to Maria

[SPD][4] research has shown that within the next eleven lines the 'dialogue' for Malvolio and the Clowne is taken from a contemporary song (see *The New Cambridge Shakespeare Twelfth Night,* page 77, footnote to lines 86-96, op. cit.): thus, the following sequences with the symbol • indicates where the modern texts suggest the lines should be sung

	Malvolio	Foole.
	Clowne	• Alas why is she so?
	Malvolio	Foole, I say.
	Clowne	• She loves another.
85		Who calles, ha?
	Malvolio	Good foole, as ever thou wilt deserve well at my hand, helpe me to a Candle, and pen, inke, and paper: as I am a Gentleman, I will live to bee thankefull to thee for't.
90	**Clowne**	M.[1] Malvolio?
	Malvolio	I good Foole.
	Clowne	Alas sir, how fell you besides your five witts?
	Malvolio	Foole, there was never man so notoriouslie a- bus'd: I am as well in my wits (foole) as thou art.
95	**Clowne**	But as well: then you are mad indeede, if you be no better in your wits then a foole.
	Malvolio	They have heere propertied me: keepe mee in darkenesse, send Ministers to me, Asses, and doe all they can to face me out of my wits.
100	**Clowne**	Advise you what you say: the Minister is heere. [2]
		{as Sir Topas} Malvolio, Malvolio, thy wittes the heavens restore: en- deavour† thy selfe to sleepe, and leave thy vaine bibble babble.
	Malvolio	Sir Topas.
105	**Clowne**	{as Sir Topas} Maintaine no words with him good fellow.
		{as self]} Who I sir, not I sir.
		God buy you good sir Topas: {as Sir Topas} Mar- ry Amen.
		{as self} I will sir, I will.

AB/W [1] most modern texts set Ff's 'M' as 'Master': however, *The Oxford Textual Companion* (op. cit.) suggests 'Monsieur' might be more appropriate (page 422, footnote to line 4.2.86)

ADD [2] instead of adding five footnotes to indicate which character the Clowne is presenting, unlike Ff this script will add bracketed character notes to the body of the text

110	**Malvolio**	Foole, foole, foole I say.
	Clowne	Alas sir be patient.
		What say you sir, I am shent
		for speaking to you.
	Malvolio	Good foole, helpe me to some light, and some
115		paper, I tell thee I am as well in my wittes, as any man in
		Illyria.
	Clowne	Well-a-day, that you were sir.
	Malvolio	By this hand I am: good foole, some inke, pa-
		per, and light: and convey what I will set downe to my
120		Lady: it shall advantage thee more, then ever the bea-
		ring of Letter did.
	Clowne	I will help you too't.
		But tel me true, are you not
		mad indeed, or do you but counterfeit.
125	**Malvolio**	Beleeve me I am not, I tell thee true.
	Clowne	Nay, Ile nere beleeve a madman till I see his brains [1]
		I will fetch you light, and paper, and inke.
	Malvolio	Foole, Ile requite it in the highest degree:
		I prethee be gone. [†2]
130	**Clowne**	I am gone sir,° and anon sir,°
		Ile be with you againe: °
		In a trice,° like to the old vice,°
		your neede to sustaine. °
		Who with dagger of lath,° in his rage and his wrath,°
135		cries ah ha,° to the divell: °
		Like a mad lad,° paire thy nayles dad,°
		Adieu good man divell. °[3]

[Exit]

[PCT]1 F1 sets no punctuation as if the two ideas run together: F2 set a comma, most modern texts a period

[W]2 F2 and modern texts = 'gone', F1 = 'goue'

[SPD]3 though not set in the italicised font normally associated with songs and poems, the text is not laid out
in the pattern usually used for spoken texts, prose or verse: there is no known song for these lines,
nevertheless, most modern texts indicate that this should be sung, and some further split the text according
to the inner rhyme scheme, as the symbols ° show

Scæna Tertia

ENTER SEBASTIAN

This is the ayre, that is the glorious Sunne,
This pearle she gave me, I do feel't, and see't,
And though tis wonder that enwraps me thus,   R 271 - b
Yet 'tis not madnesse.
                    Where's Anthonio†1 then,
5 I could not finde him at the Elephant,
Yet there he was, and† there I found this credite,
That he did range the towne to seeke me out,
His councell now might do me golden service,
10 For though my soule disputes well with my sence,
That this may be some error, but no madnesse,
Yet doth this accident and flood of Fortune,
So farre exceed all instance, all discourse,
That I am readie to distrust mine eyes,
15 And wrangle with my reason that perswades me
To any other trust, but that I am mad,
Or else the Ladies mad ; yet if 'twere so,
She could not sway her house, command her followers,
Take, and give backe affayres, and their 2 dispatch,
20 With such a smooth, discreet, and stable bearing
As I perceive she do's : there's something in't
That is deceiveable.
                    But heere the Lady comes.

ENTER OLIVIA, AND PRIEST

Olivia   Blame not this haste of mine : if you meane well
25 Now go with me, and with this holy man
Into the Chantry by : there before him,
And underneath that consecrated roofe,
Plight me the full assurance of your faith,
That my most jealious, and too doubtfull soule
30 May live at peace.

R 271 - b / L 272 - b : 4. 3. 1 - 28

w 1 F1 = 'Authonio', F2/most modern texts = 'Anthonio'

w 2 though most modern texts agree with Ff and print this as 'their', one gloss = 'them'

He shall conceale it,
Whiles you are willing it shall come to note,
What time we will our celebration keepe
According to my birth, what do you say?

35   **Sebastian**   Ile follow this good man, and go with you,
And having sworne truth, ever will be true.

Olivia   Then lead the way good father, & heavens so shine,
That they may fairely note this acte of mine.

[Exeunt]
[Finis Actus Quartus]

Actus Quintus. Scena Prima

ENTER CLOWNE AND FABIAN

	Fabian	Now as thou lov'st me, let me see his Letter.
	Clowne	Good M. Fabian, grant me another request.
	Fabian	Any thing.
	Clowne	Do not desire to see this Letter.
5	**Fabian**	This is to give a dogge, and in recompence desire my dogge againe.

ENTER DUKE, VIOLA, CURIO, AND LORDS

	Duke	Belong you to the Lady Olivia, friends?
	Clowne	I sir, we are some of her trappings.
10	**Duke**	I know thee well: how doest thou my good Fellow?
	Clowne	Truely sir, the better for my foes, and the worse for my friends.
	Duke	Just the contrary: the better for thy friends.
	Clowne	No sir, the worse.
15	**Duke**	How can that be?
	Clowne	Marry sir, they praise me, and make an asse of me, now my foes tell me plainly, I am an Asse: so that by my foes sir, I profit in the knowledge of my selfe, and by my friends I am abused: so that conclusions to be as kisses, if
20		your foure negatives make your two affirmatives, why then the worse for my friends, and the better for my foes. L 272 - b
	Duke	Why this is excellent.

	Clowne	By my troth sir, no: though it please you to be one of my friends.
25	Duke	Thou shalt not be the worse for me, there's gold.
	Clowne	But that it would be double dealing sir, I would you could make it another.
	Duke	O you give me ill counsell.
30	Clowne	Put your grace in your pocket sir, for this once, and let your flesh and blood obey it.
	Duke	Well, I will be so much a sinner to be a double dealer: there's another.
35	Clowne	*Primo, secundo, tertio,* is a good play, and the olde saying is, the third payes for all: the triplex sir, is a good tripping measure, or the belles of S. Bennet sir, may put you in minde, one, two, three.
40	Duke	You can foole no more money out of mee at this throw: if you will let your Lady know I am here to speak with her, and bring her along with you, it may awake my bounty further.
45	Clowne	Marry sir, lullaby to your bountie till I come a-gen. I go sir, but I would not have you to thinke, that my desire of having is the sinne of covetousnesse: but as you say sir, let your bounty take a nappe, I will awake it anon.

[Exit]
ENTER ANTHONIO AND OFFICERS

	Viola	Here comes the man sir, that did rescue mee.
50	Duke	That face of his I do remember well, yet [1] when I saw it last, it was besmear'd As blacke as Vulcan, in the smoake of warre: A bawbling Vessell was he Captaine of, For shallow draught and bulke unprizable, With which such scathfull grapple did he make, With the most noble bottome of our Fleete,
55		That very envy, and the tongue of losse Cride fame and honor on him: What's the matter?

R 272 - b : 5. 1. 25 - 59

COMP/VP [1] F2 and most modern texts set a capital 'Y' and thus maintain the verse: F1 sets a small 'y'

1st Officer	Orsino, this is that Anthonio
	That tooke the Phoenix, and her fraught from Candy,
	And this is he that did the Tiger boord,
60	When your yong Nephew Titus lost his legge;
	Heere in the streets, desperate of shame and state,
	In private brabble did we apprehend him.
Viola	He did me kindnesse sir, drew on my side,
	But in conclusion put strange speech upon me,
65	I know not what 'twas, but distraction.
Duke	Notable Pyrate, thou salt-water Theefe,
	What foolish boldnesse brought thee to their mercies,
	Whom thou in termes so bloudie, and so deere
	Hast made thine enemies?

70 **Antonio**

Orsino: Noble sir,
Be pleas'd that I shake off these names you give mee:
Anthonio never yet was Theefe, or Pyrate,
Though I confesse, on base and ground enough
Orsino's enemie.

75   A witchcraft drew me hither:
That most ingratefull boy there by your side,
From the rude seas enrag'd and foamy mouth
Did I redeeme: a wracke past hope he was:
His life I gave him, and did thereto adde
80 My love without retention, or restraint,
All his in dedication.
                For his sake,
Did I expose my selfe (pure for his love)
Into the danger of this adverse Towne,
85 Drew to defend him, when he was beset:
Where being apprehended, his false cunning
(Not meaning to partake with me in danger)
Taught him to face me out of his acquaintance,   R 272 - b
And grew a twentie yeeres removed thing
90 While one would winke: denide me mine owne purse,
Which I had recommended to his use,

	Not halfe an houre before.
Viola	How can this be?
Duke	When came he to this Towne? [1]

[SP][1] the actor has choice as to which two of these three short lines may be joined as one line of split verse

95	**Antonio**	To day my Lord: and for three months before,
		No *intrim*, not a minutes vacancie,
		Both day and night did we keepe companie.

ENTER OLIVIA AND ATTENDANTS

	Duke	Heere comes the Countesse, now heaven walkes
		on earth:
100		But for thee fellow, fellow thy words are madnesse,
		Three monthes this youth hath tended upon mee,
		But more of that anon.
		Take him aside.

	Olivia	What would my Lord, but that he may not have,
105		Wherein Olivia may seeme serviceable?
		Cesario, you do not keepe promise with me.

	Viola	Madam:
	Duke	Gracious Olivia. * [1]
	Olivia	What do you say Cesario?
110		Good my Lord. *
	Viola	My Lord would speake, my dutie hushes me.
	Olivia	If it be ought to the old tune my Lord,
		It is as fat and fulsome to mine eare

> | | | |
> |---|---|---|
> | | | As howling after Musicke. |
> | 115 | **Duke** | Still so cruell? |
> | | **Olivia** | Still so constant Lord. [2] |

	Duke	What to perversenesse? you uncivill Ladie
		To whose ingrate, and unauspicious Altars
		My soule the faithfull'st offrings have [3] breath'd out
120		That ere devotion tender'd.
		What shall I do?
	Olivia	Even what it please my Lord, that shal becom him [4]

[PCT] [1] here and several times through the remainder of the scene modern texts replace a period set by Ff with a dash, suggesting the next character interrupts the one now speaking : to save frequent footnotes, all such subsequent resettings in this scene will be marked with the symbol * without an accompanying footnote

[SP] [2] the actor has choice as to which two of these three short lines may be joined as one line of split verse

[W] [3] most modern texts = 'hath' or 'has', Ff = 'have'

[PCT] [4] F1 seems to suggest that Orsino interrupts Olivia, though the peculiar line ('shal becom him' with no punctuation) almost certainly stems from lack of column width : F2 = 'shall becom/(him', with the him set on the line above flanked by an opening bracket: most modern texts = 'shall become him.'

Duke		Why should I not, (had I the heart to do it)
		Like to th'Egyptian theefe, at point of death
125		Kill what I love: (a savage jealousie,
		That sometime savours nobly) but heare me this:
		Since you to non-regardance cast my faith,
		And that I partly know the instrument
		That screwes me from my true place in your favour:
130		Live you the Marble-brested Tirant still.

But this your Minion, whom I know you love,
And whom, by heaven I sweare, I tender deerely,
Him will I teare out of that cruell eye,
Where he sits crowned in his masters spight.

135   Come boy with me, my thoughts are ripe in mischiefe:
Ile sacrifice the Lambe that I do love,
To spight a Ravens heart within a Dove. [1]

Viola   And I most jocund, apt, and willinglie,
To do you rest, a thousand deaths would dye. [2]

140   **Olivia**   Where goes Cesario?
                      }

Viola   After him I love,
More then I love these eyes, more then my life,
More by all mores, then ere I shall love wife.

If I do feigne, you witnesses above
145   Punish my life, for tainting of my love.

Olivia   Aye me detested, how am I beguil'd?

Viola   Who does beguile you? who does do you wrong?

Olivia   Hast thou forgot thy selfe?
                    Is it so long?

150   Call forth the holy Father. [3]
                      }

Duke   Come, away.

Olivia   Whether my Lord?
            Cesario, Husband, stay.

[SD]1 most modern texts suggest that Orsino now starts to leave

[SD]2 most modern texts suggest that Viola now starts to follow Orsino

[SD]3 most modern texts add a stage direction that one of Olivia's Attendants leaves to fetch the Priest

Duke	Husband?	

155 **Olivia** I Husband.
⟩
Can he that deny?

Duke Her husband, sirrah?

Viola No my Lord, not I.
⟩

Olivia Alas, it is the basenesse of thy feare, L 273-b
160 That makes thee strangle thy propriety:
Feare not Cesario, take thy fortunes up,
Be that thou know'st thou art, and then thou art
As great as that thou fear'st.

ENTER PRIEST

O welcome Father:
165 Father, I charge thee by thy reverence
Heere to unfold, though lately we intended
To keepe in darknesse, what occasion now
Reveales before 'tis ripe: what thou dost know
Hath newly past, betweene this youth, and me.

170 **Priest** A Contract of eternall bond of love,
Confirm'd by mutuall joynder of your hands,
Attested by the holy close of lippes,
Strengthned by enterchangement of your rings,
And all the Ceremonie of this compact
175 Seal'd in my function, by my testimony:
Since when, my watch hath told me, toward my grave
I have travail'd but two houres.

Duke O thou dissembling Cub: what wilt thou be
When time hath sow'd a grizzle on thy case?
180 Or will not else thy craft so quickely grow,
That thine owne trip shall be thine overthrow:
Farewell, and take her, but direct thy feete,
Where thou, and I (henceforth) may never meet.

Viola My Lord, I do protest. *
⟩
185 **Olivia** O do not sweare,
Hold little faith, though thou hast too much feare.

ENTER SIR ANDREW [1]

L 273-b / R 273-b : 5. 1. 145 - 171

[SD1] most modern texts add to the stage direction that Andrew's head is bleeding

92

	Andrew	For the love of God a Surgeon, send one pre- sently to sir Toby.
	Olivia	What's the matter?
190	**Andrew**	H'as broke my head a-crosse, and has given Sir Toby a bloody Coxcombe too: for the love of God your helpe, I had rather then forty pound I were at home. †1
	Olivia	Who has done this sir Andrew?
195	**Andrew**	The Counts Gentleman, one Cesario: we tooke him for a Coward, but hee's the verie divell incardinate†2.
	Duke	My Gentleman Cesario?
	Andrew	Odd's lifelings heere he is: you broke my head for nothing, and that that I did, I was set on to do't by sir Toby.
200	**Viola**	Why do you speake to me, I never hurt you: ³ you drew your sword upon me without cause, But I bespake you faire and hurt you not.

ENTER TOBY AND CLOWNE

	Andrew	If a bloody coxcombe be a hurt, you have hurt me: I thinke you set nothing by a bloody Coxecombe.
205		Heere comes sir Toby halting, you shall heare more: but if he had not beene in drinke, hee would have tickel'd you other gates then he did.
	Duke	How now Gentleman? how ist with you?
210	**Toby**	That's all one, has hurt me, and there's th'end on't: Sot, didst see Dicke Surgeon, sot?
	Clowne	O he's drunke sir Toby an houre agone: his eyes were set at eight i'th morning.
	Toby	Then he's a Rogue, and a passy measures panyn: ⁴ I hate a drunken rogue.

R 273 - b : 5. 1. 172 - 201

ᵂ 1 F2 and most modern texts = 'home', F1 = 'homc'

ᵂ 2 F2 and most modern texts = 'incardinate', F1 = 'incardinatc'

ᶜᴼᴹᴾ/ⱽᴾ 3 following Andrew's entry everybody else speaks prose, save Viola: here F1 is the only text to set a
small 'y': F2 and most modern texts set a capital 'Y', thus maintaining her speech as verse throughout (see
footnote #7 page 53)

ᵂ 4 F2 and most modern texts = 'pavin', F1 = 'panyn'

215	**Olivia**	Away with him? who hath made this havocke with them?	
	Andrew	Ile helpe you sir Toby, because we'll be drest to-gether.	
220	**Toby**	Will you helpe an Asse-head,[1] and a coxcombe, & a knave: a thin fac'd knave, a gull?	R 273 - b
	Olivia	Get him to bed, and let his hurt be look'd too.[2]	

ENTER SEBASTIAN

	Sebastian	I am sorry Madam I have hurt your kinsman: But had it beene the brother of my blood, I must have done no lesse with wit and safety.
225		You throw a strange regard upon me, and by that I do perceive it hath offended you: Pardon me (sweet one) even for the vowes We made each other, but so late ago.
230	**Duke**	One face, one voice, one habit, and two persons, A naturall Perspective, that is, and is not.
	Sebastian	Anthonio: O my deere Anthonio, How have the houres rack'd, and tortur'd me, Since I have lost thee?
	Antonio	Sebastian are you?
235	**Sebastian**	Fear'st thou that Anthonio?[3]
	Antonio	How have you made division of your selfe, An apple cleft in two, is not more twin Then these two creatures. Which is Sebastian?
240	**Olivia**	Most wonderfull.

[PCT 1] the only conclusion from this unpunctuated Ff phrase is that Toby is calling himself an 'Asse-head': however, most modern texts add some form of punctuation thus separating 'Will you helpe' from 'an Asse-head'; the resulting implication is that Toby is now attacking Andrew instead of himself: (for the enormous implications of this unwarranted rewrite, see Freeman, Neil H.M. *Shakespeare's First Texts*. Vancouver, 1994. Pages 6-7

[SD 2] most modern texts provide an exit for Andrew, Toby, the Clowne and Fabian

[SP 3] the actor has choice as to which two of these three short lines may be joined as one line of split verse

Sebastian	Do I stand there?
	I never had a brother:
	Nor can there be that Deity in my nature
	Of heere, and every where.
	I had a sister,
	Whom the blinde waves and surges have devour'd:
	Of charity, what kinne are you to me?
	What Countreyman?
	What name?
	What Parentage?
Viola	Of Messaline: Sebastian was my Father,
	Such a Sebastian was my brother too:
	So went he suited to his watery tombe:
	If spirits can assume both forme and suite,
	You come to fright us.
Sebastian	A spirit I am indeed,
	But am in that dimension grossely clad,
	Which from the wombe I did participate.
	Were you a woman, as the rest goes even,
	I should my teares let fall upon your cheeke,
	And say, thrice welcome drowned Viola.
Viola	My father had a moale upon his brow.
Sebastian	And so had mine.
Viola	And dide that day when Viola from her birth
	Had numbred thirteene yeares.
Sebastian	O that record is lively in my soule,
	He finished indeed his mortall acte
	That day that made my sister thirteene yeares.
Viola	If nothing lets to make us happie both,
	But this my masculine usurp'd attyre:
	Do not embrace me, till each circumstance,
	Of place, time, fortune, do co-here and jumpe
	That I am Viola, which to confirme,
	Ile bring you to a Captaine in this Towne,
	Where lye my maiden weeds: by whose gentle helpe,
	I was preserv'd to serve this Noble Count:
	All the occurrence of my fortune since
	Hath beene betweene this Lady, and this Lord.

Sebastian	So comes it Lady, you have beene mistooke:	
280	But Nature to her bias drew in that.	
	You would have bin contracted to a Maid,	
	Nor are you therein (by my life) deceiv'd,	
	You are betroth'd both to a maid and man.	
Duke	¹ Be not amaz'd, right noble is his blood:	
285	If this be so, as yet the glasse seemes true,	
	I shall have share in this most happy wracke,	
	Boy, thou hast saide to me a thousand times,	
	Thou never should'st love woman like to me.	
Viola	And all those sayings, will I over sweare,	
290	And all those swearings keepe as true in soule,	L 274 - b
	As doth that Orbed Continent, the fire,	
	That severs day from†² night.	

Duke | Give me thy hand,
And let me see thee in thy womans weedes.

295 Viola | The Captaine that did bring me first on shore
Hath my Maides garments: he upon some Action
Is now in durance, at Malvolio's suite,
A Gentleman, and follower of my Ladies.

Olivia | He shall inlarge him: fetch Malvolio hither,
300 | And yet alas, now I remember me,
They say poore Gentleman, he's much distract.

ENTER CLOWNE WITH A LETTER, AND FABIAN

A most extracting ³ frensie of mine owne
From my remembrance, clearly banisht his.
How does he sirrah?

305 Clowne | Truely Madam, he holds Belzebub at the staves end as
well as a man in his case may do: has heere writ a letter to
you, I should have given't you to day morning. But as a
madmans Epistles are no Gospels, so it skilles not much
310 | when they are deliver'd.

Olivia | Open't, and read it.

ᵂᴴᴼ ¹ most modern texts suggest the first three lines are spoken to Olivia, the remainder to Viola

ᵂ ² F2 and most modern texts = 'from', F1 = 'ftom'

ᵂ ³ F1 = 'extracting', F2 = 'exacting', one modern gloss = 'distracting'

Clowne		Looke then to be well edified, when the Foole delivers the Madman.
		[1] *By the Lord Madam.*
315	**Olivia**	How now, art thou mad?
	Clowne	No Madam, I do but reade madnesse: and your Ladyship will have it as it ought to bee, you must allow *Vox.*
	Olivia	Prethee reade i'thy right wits.
320	**Clowne**	So I do Madona: but to reade his right wits, is to reade thus: therefore, perpend my Princesse, and give eare.
	Olivia	Read it you, sirrah.
	Fabian [Reads] [2]	By the Lord Madam, you wrong me, and
325		the world shall know it: Though you have put mee into darkenesse, and given your drunken Cosine rule over me, yet have I the benefit of my senses as well as your Ladie-ship.
330		I have your owne letter, that induced mee to the semblance I put on; with the which I doubt not, but to do my selfe much right, or you much shame: thinke of me as you please.
		I leave my duty a little unthought of, and speake out of my injury.
335		*The madly us'd Malvolio.*
	Olivia	Did he write this?
	Clowne	I Madame.
	Duke	This savours not much of distraction.
340	**Olivia**	See him deliver'd Fabian, bring him hither: [3] My Lord, so please you, these things further thought on, To thinke me as well a sister, as a wife, One day shall crowne th'alliance on't, so please you, Heere at my house, and at my proper cost.

SD 1 most modern texts add a stage direction that he reads in a 'mad' fashion

COMP 2 though when the Clowne began to read the letter, the normal Ff italicised font usually associated with letters was set, as Fabian reads, the letter is set in the type face usually associated with just dialogue: whether this has any implication for the reading of the letter is up to each reader to decide

SD 3 most modern texts add a stage direction for Fabian's exit

Duke		Madam, I am most apt t'embrace your offer:
345	¹	Your Master quits you: and for your service done him,
		So much against the mettle of your sex,
		So farre beneath your soft and tender breeding,
		And since you call'd me Master, for so long:
		Heere is my hand, you shall from this time bee
350	²	your Masters Mistris.
		}
Olivia	³	A sister, you are she.

ENTER MALVOLIO

Duke	Is this the Madman?
Olivia	I my Lord, this same: ° How now Malvolio?
Malvolio	Madam, you have done me wrong, ° ⁴

355	Notorious wrong.
	}
Olivia	Have I Malvolio?
	No.

Malvolio	Lady you have, pray you peruse that Letter.
	You must not now denie it is your hand,
360	Write from it if you can, in hand, or phrase,
	Or say, tis not your seale, not your invention:
	You can say none of this.
	Well, grant it then,
	And tell me in the modestie of honor,
365	Why you have given me such cleare lights of favour,
	Bad me come smiling, and crosse-garter'd to you,
	To put on yellow stockings, and to frowne
	Upon sir Toby, and the lighter people:
	And acting this in an obedient hope,
370	Why have you suffer'd me to be imprison'd,
	Kept in a darke house, visited by the Priest,
	And made the most notorious gecke and gull,
	That ere invention plaid on?
	Tell me why?

R 274 - b

R 274 - b / L 275 - b : 5. 1. 320 - 344

WHO ¹ most modern texts indicate this is spoken to Viola

COMP/VP ² F2 and most modern texts set a capital 'Y', thus maintaining the verse: F1 sets a small 'y'

W ³ though most modern texts agree with Ff and print this as 'A', one gloss = 'Ah'

LS ⁴ the irregular setting of Ff (5/10 or 11/7 syllables) allows due weight for the reaction to Malvolio's entry before anyone can speak, and a pause for him before he can start: the regularising of the modern texts (10/12 or 13) creates overblown passion on the second line where none existed before

375	Olivia	Alas Malvolio, this is not my writing,
		Though I confesse much like the Charracter:
		But out of question, tis Marias hand.

And now I do bethinke me, it was shee
First told me thou wast mad; then cam'st in smiling,
380 And in such formes, which heere were presuppos'd
Upon thee in the Letter: prethee be content,
This practice hath most shrewdly past upon thee:
But when we know the grounds, and authors of it,
Thou shalt be both the Plaintiffe and the Judge
385 Of thine owne cause.

Fabian Good Madam heare me speake,
And let no quarrell, nor no braule to come,
Taint the condition of this present houre,
Which I have wondred at.
390   In hope it shall not,
Most freely I confesse my selfe, and Toby
Set this device against Malvolio heere,
Upon some stubborne and uncourteous parts
We had conceiv'd against him.
395   Maria writ
The Letter, at sir Tobyes great importance,
In recompence whereof, he hath married her:
How with a sportfull malice it was follow'd,
May rather plucke on laughter then revenge,
400 If that the injuries be justly weigh'd,
That have on both sides past.

Olivia Alas poore Foole, how have they baffel'd thee?

Clowne Why some are borne great, some atchieve greatnesse, and some have greatnesse throwne upon them.
405   I
was one sir, in this Enterlude, one sir Topas sir, but that's   L 275 - b
all one: By the Lord[1] Foole, I am not mad: but do you remember, Madam, why laugh you at such a barren rascall,
and you smile not he's gag'd: and thus the whirlegigge
410 of time, brings in his revenges.

Malvolio Ile be reveng'd on the whole packe of you?[2]

Olivia He hath bene most notoriously abus'd.

L 275 - b / R 275 - b : 5. 1. 345 - 379

[1] F2 and most modern texts = 'Lord', F1 = 'Lotd'
[2] most modern texts add a stage direction here for Malvolio's exit

99

Duke	Pursue him, and entreate him to a peace :
	He hath not told us of the Captaine yet,[1]
415	When that is knowne, and golden time convents
	A solemne Combination shall be made
	Of our deere soules.

          Meane time sweet sister,
We will not part from hence.

420   Cesario come
(For so you shall be while you are a man :)
But when in other habites you are seene,
Orsino's Mistris, and his fancies Queene.

[Exeunt] [2]

Clowne sings

When that I was and a little tine boy,
 with hey, ho, the winde and the raine :
A foolish thing was but a toy,
 for the raine it raineth every day.

But when I came to mans estate,
 with hey ho, &c.
Gainst Knaves and Theeves men shut their gate,
 for the raine, &c.

But when I came alas to wive,
 with hey ho, &c.
By swaggering could I never thrive,
 for the raine, &c.

But when I came unto my beds,
 with hey ho, &c.
With tospottes still had drunken heades,
 for the raine, &c.

A great while ago the world begon ,[3]
 [4] *hey ho, &c.*
But that's all one, our Play is done,
 and wee'l strive to please you every day. [5]

425 (line with "raine")
430 (line with "gate")
435 (line with "thrive")
440 (line with "begon")

SD[1] most modern texts add a stage direction here for someone, possibly from the Duke's retinue, or sometimes Fabian, to go after Malvolio

SD[2] most modern texts suggest the exit is for everyone except the Clowne

W[3] most modern texts = 'begun', Ff = 'begon'

W[4] most modern texts add 'with', Ff omit the word

SD[5] most modern texts add an exit for the Clowne

FINIS

R 275 - b

APPENDIX A
THE UNEASY RELATIONSHIP OF FOLIO,
QUARTOS, AND MODERN TEXTS

Between the years 1590 and 1611, one William Shakespeare, a playwright and actor, delivered to the company of which he was a major shareholder at least thirty-seven plays in handwritten manuscript form. Since the texts belonged to the company upon delivery, he derived no extra income from publishing them. Indeed, as far as scholars can establish, he took no interest in the publication of his plays.

Consequently, without his supervision, yet during his lifetime and shortly after, several different publishers printed eighteen of these plays, each in separate editions. Each of these texts, known as **'Quartos'** because of the page size and method of folding each printed sheet, was about the size of a modern hardback novel. In 1623, seven years after Shakespeare's death, Heminges and Condell, two friends, theatrical colleagues, actors, and fellow shareholders in the company, passed on to the printer, William Jaggard, the handwritten copies of not only these eighteen plays but a further eighteen, of which seventeen had been performed but not yet seen in print.[1] These thirty-six plays were issued in one large volume, each page about the size of a modern legal piece of paper. Anything printed in this larger format was known as 'folio', again because of the page size and the method of sheet folding. Thus the 1623 printing of the collected works is known as **the First Folio,** its 1632 reprint (with more than 1600 unauthorised corrections) the Second Folio, and the next reprint, the 1666 Third Folio, added the one missing play, *Pericles* (which had been set in quarto and performed).

The handwritten manuscript used for the copies of the texts from which both Quartos and the First Folio were printed came from a variety of sources. Closest to Shakespeare were those in his own hand, known as the 'foul papers' because of the natural blottings, crossings out, and corrections. Sometimes he had time to pass the material on to a manuscript copyist who would make a clean copy, known as the 'fair papers'. Whether fair (if there was sufficient time) or foul (if the performance deadline was close), the papers would be passed on to the Playhouse, where a 'Playhouse copy' would be made, from which the 'sides' (individual copies of each part with just a single cue line) would be prepared for each actor. Whether Playhouse copy, fair papers, or foul, the various Elizabethan and Jacobean handwritten manuscripts from which the quartos and Folio came have long since disappeared.

The first printed texts of the Shakespeare plays were products of a speaking-

---

[1]   Though written between 1605–09, *Timon of Athens* was not performed publicly until 1761.

hearing society. They were based on rhetoric, a verbal form of arranging logic and argument in a persuasive, pleasing, and entertaining fashion so as to win personal and public debates, a system which allowed individuals to express at one and the same time the steppingstones in an argument while releasing the underlying emotional feelings that accompanied it.[2] Naturally, when ideas were set on paper they mirrored this same form of progression in argument and the accompanying personal release, allowing both neat and untidy thoughts to be seen at a glance (see the General Introduction, pp. xvi–xxi). Thus what was set on paper was not just a silent debate. It was at the same time a reminder of how the human voice might be heard both logically and passionately in that debate.

Such reminders did not last into the eighteenth century. Three separate but interrelated needs insisted on cleaning up the original printings so that silent and speaking reader alike could more easily appreciate the beauties of one of England's greatest geniuses.

First, by 1700, publishing's main thrust was to provide texts to be read privately by people of taste and learning. Since grammar was now the foundation for all writing, publication, and reading, all the Elizabethan and early Jacobean material still based on rhetoric appeared at best archaic and at worst incomprehensible. All printing followed the new universality of grammatical and syntactical standards, standards which still apply today. Consequently any earlier book printed prior to the establishment of these standards had to be reshaped in order to be understood. And the Folio/Quarto scripts, even the revamped versions which had already begun to appear, presented problems in this regard, especially when dealing in the moments of messy human behaviour. Thus, while the first texts were reshaped according to the grammatical knowledge of the 1700s, much of the shaping of the rhetoric was (inadvertently) removed from the plays.

Secondly, the more Shakespeare came to be recognized as a literary poet rather than as a theatrical genius, the less the plays were likely to be considered as performance texts. Indeed plot lines of several of his plays were altered (or ignored) to satisfy the more refined tastes of the period. And the resultant demands for poetic and literary clarity, as well as those of grammar, altered the first printings even further.

Thirdly, scholars argued a need for revision of both Quarto and Folio texts because of 'interfering hands' (hands other than Shakespeare's) having had undue influence on the texts. No matter whether foul or fair papers or Playhouse copy, so the argument ran, several intermediaries would be involved between Shakespeare's writ-

---

[2] For an extraordinarily full analysis of the art of rhetoric, readers are guided to Sister Miriam Joseph, *Shakespeare's Use of the Arts of Language* (New York: Haffner Publishing Co., 1947). For a more theatrical overview, readers are directed to Bertram Joseph, *Acting Shakespeare* (New York: Theatre Arts Books, 1960). For an overview involving aspects of Ff/Qq, readers are immodestly recommended to Neil Freeman, *Shakespeare's First Texts*, op. cit.

ing of the plays and the printing of them. If the fair papers provided the source text, a copyist might add some peculiarities, as per the well documented Ralph Crane.[3] If the Playhouse copy was the source text, extra information, mainly stage directions, would have been added by someone other than Shakespeare, turning the play from a somewhat literary document into a performance text. Finally, while more than five different compositors were involved in setting the First Folio, five did the bulk of the printing house work: each would have their individual pattern of typesetting — compositor E being singled out as far weaker than the rest. Thus between Shakespeare and the printed text might lie the hand(s) of as few as one and as many as three other people, even more when more than one compositor set an individual play. Therefore critics argue because there is the chance of so much interference between Shakespearean intent and the first printings of the plays, the plays do not offer a stylistic whole, i.e., while the words themselves are less likely to be interfered with, their shapings, the material consistently altered in the early 1700s, are not that of a single hand, and thus cannot be relied upon.

These well-intentioned grammatical and poetic alterations may have introduced Shakespeare to a wider reading audience, but their unforeseen effect was to remove the Elizabethan flavour of argument and of character development (especially in the areas of stress and the resulting textual irregularities), thus watering down and removing literally thousands of rhetorical and theatrical clues that those first performance scripts contained. And it is from this period that the division between ancient and modern texts begins. As a gross generalisation, the first texts, the First Folio and the quartos, could be dubbed 'Shakespeare for the stage'; the second, revamped early 1700 texts 'Shakespeare for the page'.

And virtually all current editions are based on the page texts of the early 1700s. While the words of each play remain basically the same, what shapes them, their sentences, punctuation, spelling, capitalisation, and sometimes even line structure, is often altered, unwittingly destroying much of their practical theatrical value.

It is important to neither condemn the modern editions nor blindly accept the authority of the early stage texts as gospel. This is not a case of 'old texts good, so modern texts bad'. The modern texts are of great help in literary and historical research, especially as to the meanings of obscure words and phrases, and in explaining literary allusions and historical events. They offer guidance to alternative text readings made by reputed editors, plus sound grammatical readings of difficult pas-

---

[3] Though not of the theatre (his principle work was to copy material for lawyers) Crane was involved in the preparation of at least five plays in the Folio, as well as two plays for Thomas Middleton. Scholars characterise his work as demonstrating regular and careful scene and act division, though he is criticised for his heavy use of punctuation and parentheses, apostrophes and hyphens, and 'massed entry' stage directions, i.e. where all the characters with entrances in the scene are listed in a single direction at the top of the scene irrespective of where they are supposed to enter.

sages and clarification of errors that appear in the first printings.[4] In short, they can give the starting point of the play's journey, an understanding of the story, and the conflict between characters within the story. But they can only go so far.

They cannot give you fully the conflict within each character, the very essence for the fullest understanding of the development and resolution of any Shakespeare play. Thanks to their rhetorical, theatrical base the old texts add this vital extra element. They illustrate with great clarity the 'ever-changing present' (see p. xvi in the General Introduction) in the intellectual and emotional life of each character; their passages of harmony and dysfunction, and transitions between such passages; the moments of their personal costs or rewards; and their sensual verbal dance of debate and release. In short, the old texts clearly demonstrate the essential elements of living, breathing, reacting humanity—especially in times of joyous or painful stress.

By presenting the information contained in the First Folio, together with modern restructurings, both tested against theatrical possibilities, these texts should go far in bridging the gap between the two different points of view.

---

[4] For example, the peculiar phrase 'a Table of greene fields' assigned to Mistress Quickly in describing the death of Falstaffe, *Henry V* (Act Two, Scene 3), has been superbly diagnosed as a case of poor penmanship being badly transcribed: the modern texts wisely set 'a babbled of green fields' instead.

NEIL FREEMAN trained as an actor at the Bristol Old Vic Theatre School. He has acted and directed in England, Canada, and the USA. Currently he is an Head of Graduate Directing and Senior Acting Professor in the Professional Training Programme of the Department of Theatre, Film, and Creative Writing at the University of British Columbia. He also teaches regularly at the National Theatre School of Canada, Concordia University, Brigham Young University in both Provo and Hawaii, and is on the teaching faculty of professional workshops in Montreal, Toronto and Vancouver. He is associated with Shakespeare & Co. in Lenox; the Will Geer Theatre in Los Angeles; Bard on the Beach in Vancouver; Repercussion Theatre in Montreal; and has worked with the Stratford Festival, Canada, and Shakespeare Santa Cruz.

His ground breaking work in using the first printings of the Shakespeare texts in performance, on the rehearsal floor and in the classroom has lead to lectures at the Shakespeare Association of America and workshops at both the ATHE and VASTA, and grants/fellowships from the National Endowment of the Arts (USA), The Social Science and Humanities Research Council (Canada), and York University in Toronto.

His three collations of Shakespeare and music - *A Midsummer Nights Dream* (for three actors, chorus, and Orchestra); *If This Be Love* (for three actors, mezzo-soprano, and Orchestra); *The Four Seasons of Shakespeare and Vivaldi* (for two actors, violin soloist and Chamber Orchestra) - commissioned and performed by Bard On The Beach and The Vancouver Symphony Orchestra have been received with great public acclaim.

THE ACTOR AND THE TEXT
by Cicely Berry

As voice director of the Royal Shakespeare Company, Cicely Berry has worked with actors such as Jeremy Irons, Derek Jacobi, Jonathan Pryce, Sinead Cusack and Antony Sher. *The Actor and The Text* brings Ms. Berry's methods of applying vocal production skills within a text to the general public.

While this book focuses primarily on speaking Shakespeare, Ms. Berry also includes the speaking of some modern playwrights, such as Edward Bond.

As Ms. Berry describes her own volume in the introduction:

" ... this book is not simply about making the voice sound more interesting. It is about getting inside the words we use ...It is about making the language organic, so that the words act as a spur to the sound ..."

paper•ISBN 1-155783-138-6

APPLAUSE

SHAKESPEARE'S PLAYS IN PERFORMANCE
by John Russell Brown

In this volume, John Russell Brown snatches Shakespeare from the clutches of dusty academics and thrusts him centerstage where he belongs—in performance.

Brown's thorough analysis of the theatrical experience of Shakespeare forcibly demonstrates how the text is brought to life: awakened, colored, emphasized, and extended by actors and audiences, designers and directors.

"A knowledge of what precisely can and should happen when a play is performed is, for me, the essential first step towards an understanding of Shakespeare."
—*from the Introduction by John Russell Brown*

paper•ISBN 1-55783-136-X•

APPLAUSE

RECYCLING SHAKESPEARE

by Charles Marowitz

Marowitz' irreverent approach to the bard is destined to outrage Shakespearean scholars across the globe. Marowitz rejects the notion that a "classic" is a sacrosanct entity fixed in time and bounded by its text. A living classic, according to Marowitz, should provoke lively response—even indignation!

In the same way that Shakespeare himself continued to meditate and transform his own ideas and the shape they took, Marowitz gives us license to continue that meditation in productions extrapolated from Shakespeare's work. Shakespeare becomes the greatest of all catalysts who stimulates a constant re-formulation of the fundamental questions of philosophy, history and meaning. Marowitz introduces us to Shakespeare as an active contemporary collaborator who strives with us to yield a vibrant contemporary theatre.

paper • ISBN: 1-55783-094-0

APPLAUSE

SOLILOQUY!

The Shakespeare Monologues
Edited by Michael Earley and Philippa Keil

At last, over 175 of Shakespeare's finest and most performable monologues taken from all 37 plays are here in two easy-to-use volumes (MEN and WOMEN). Selections travel the entire spectrum of the great dramatist's vision, from comedies and romances to tragedies, pathos and histories.

"Soliloquy is an excellent and comprehensive collection of Shakespeare's speeches. Not only are the monologues wide-ranging and varied, but they are superbly annotated. Each volume is prefaced by an informative and reassuring introduction, which explains the signals and signposts by which Shakespeare helps an actor on his journey through the text. It includes a very good explanation of blank verse, with excellent examples of irregularities which are specifically related to character and acting intentions. These two books are a must for any actor in search of a 'classical' audition piece."

ELIZABETH SMITH
Head of Voice & Speech
The Juilliard School

paper•MEN: ISBN 0-936839-78-3
WOMEN: ISBN 0-936839-79-1

APPLAUSE

SHAKESPEARE'S FIRST TEXTS
by Neil Freeman

"THE ACTOR'S BEST CHAMPION OF THE
FOLIO"   —Kristin Linklater
                    author of *Freeing Shakespeare's Voice*

Neil Freeman provides students, scholars, theatre-lovers, and, most importantly, actors and directors, with a highly readable, illuminating, and indispensable guide to William Shakespeare's own first quill-inscribed texts — SHAKESPEARE'S FIRST TEXTS.

Four hundred years later, most of the grammatical and typographical information conveyed by this representation in Elizabethan type by the first play compositors has been lost. Or, rather, discarded, in order to conform to the new standards of usage. Granted, this permitted more readers access to Shakespeare's writing, but it also did away with some of Shakespeare himself.

ISBN 1-155783-335-4

APPLAUSE